every penny ¢ount$

Becoming a Middle-Income Millionaire

JEANNA L. PRYOR

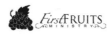

*First*FRUITS
MINISTRY

PUBLISHED BY FIRSTFRUITS MINISTRY
Copyright © 2009 by FinanceCoach Jeanna L. Pryor and FirstFruits Ministry. All
Rights Reserved

This book contains the Author's personal thoughts and beliefs that, through sound
financial budgeting and planning, individual wealth can be obtained. Although
"wealth" is an ambiguous term and can only be defined by the individual, the
Author believes individuals do not have to struggle financially and through
discipline can achieve financial wealth. The information presented is accurate at
the time of publication. However, no part of this book should be considered as the
rendering of legal, accounting, or professional financial services by the Author or
Publishers. Since finance is a personal and individual undertaking, the reader is
advised to seek certified professional assistance and advice as it specifically pertains
to his/her situation. The Author and Publishers specifically disclaim any liability,
loss, or risk which is incurred as a consequence, directly or indirectly, of the use and
application of any of the contents of this book.

Scripture references are taken from the New International Version unless noted
otherwise.

Cover design by Brandon Pryor and Makya Renée Pryor.
Typsetting by Makya Renée Pryor.

ISBN: 0-9841774-0-X

Printed in the United States of America

First Edition

This is a FirstFruits Ministry Publication.

PROLOGUE

Are you tired of living paycheck to paycheck? Are you robbing Peter to pay Paul or drowning in credit card debt? The American Bankruptcy Institute said that in the first half of 2009 bankruptcy filings are higher than at any point since bankruptcy reform in 2005, and if the pace continues, more than 1.3 million consumer bankruptcies will be filed. Business Week reports that with borrowers falling behind in mortgage and other debt payments, the next financial meltdown will come from the $950 billion worth of outstanding credit card debt, "most of it toxic". Is this you? What do you do when the money runs out before all of the bills are paid? Are you asking yourself, 'Now that I have messed up (my money and my credit) – what's next? Maybe you think, 'I've never been rich and I can't pay my bills, how do I have a happy life? *Every Penny Counts* gives you answers, tips, and techniques to end the cycle of debt, using the money you currently make.

ABOUT THE AUTHOR

I had a great childhood. I grew up in a middle-income family of five. My father was a teacher and my mother worked in the fashion design business before it became the glamorous business of today. My father was salaried, only during the school year, and my mom was paid based on how many items of clothing she finished each pay period. At times money was tight and sometimes our family struggled between paydays. To make matters worse, my father was sickly and his medical bills caused additional financial stress.

Our neighbors and family members had some of the same financial challenges we had. What eased our struggle was that we lived in a time where we helped each other out; therefore, children never went without the necessities. I remember the code word the adults used when they borrowed from one another, "the package", meant money.

Living like this caused me to focus on what I would do differently when I ventured out on my own. Times have changed, but the numbers of families that are financially struggling have not. I want to share what I've learned to make a difference in the lives of families today.

ACKNOWLEDGEMENTS

This book is the culmination of a longtime dream. It's been my passion and gift to help people get out of debt. I've been doing this on a one-on-one basis since 1982. My desire is to touch millions of lives to help people get out of financial bondage and experience the financial freedom that God intends for them to enjoy. I hope this book transforms your life and is the stepping stone to you reaching your financial dreams and financial independence.

My goal was to keep the process simple because overly-complicated budgets are usually 1) frustrating to use, 2) not used, and/or 3) not necessary. You don't have to be an accountant who uses lots of spreadsheets and ledgers to track your money. However, if you want to be financially prosperous, you have to use a budget.

I want to thank my family and friends who believed I could write this book. I've had many starts and stops along the journey, but they never gave up on me. I want to thank my husband Nehemiah for his love and support, JaNeil and Janet for editing, Brandon and Makya for designing the cover, Jeremy and Lanier for providing their candid comments. I especially want to thank Pastors Joey Elsky and Delman Coates for giving me the opportunity to teach these principles at church.

I give thatks to God for giving me this gift and allowing me to use it to change lives.

"For I know the plans I have for you," declares the Lord,
"plans to prosper you and not to harm you,
plans to give you hope and a future."
- Jeremiah 29:11

CONTENTS

every
penny
¢ount$

INTRODUCTION

Many people complain that it's tough to make ends meet. The primary reason is that many are over their heads in debt. Before they are paid, they owe most of their salary to someone for something, and in most cases, that "something" is no longer available or usable. That's unfortunate because life doesn't have to be that way.

You don't have to live a life of lack and financial stress. "If only I made more money," you might remark. In reality, however, it doesn't matter whether you earn $60,000 or $600,000 a year. The amount you earn does not guarantee financial success. You can be debt poor or financially free. What makes the difference is how you use money. My mother always said, "Baby, it's not what you make that counts, it's what you do with what you make." That was true when she was growing up and it is still true today.

Many have forgotten that there was a time, not so many decades ago, when it was uncommon to borrow. Cash was KING! Today people have come to believe that debt is good, and lots of debt is not a problem.

But as our economy swings back and forth, one saying has been proven true and has stood the test of time. "The borrower is slave to the lender." That proverb comes from King Solomon, the book of Proverbs, chapter 22, verse 7 in the bible.

The borrower is a slave or under the control of the lender because the lender sets the loan terms and can take back their property if you miss payments. The lender also can adversely affect your future when: 1) he submits credit reports, 2) he calls and hassles - even sometimes harasses – you, affecting your peace of mind, and 3) some of the credit report information impacts current and future employment opportunities. I'm sure you probably know someone who has experienced these unpleasant sides of being a borrower.

I wrote this book to provide information to help you take back power over money management and borrowing. I want to share some of the tactics lenders use and give you information to assist you to make informed buying decisions. I want to give you tools to take control of your spending and change your family's future.

Some of what I will share with you may not be new. It'll be a refresher. However, I hope most of what you read will be helpful.

First, I'll talk about some of the pitfalls of being a spender and show you how to be a saver. Just like a little spending every day can rob you of your dreams, saving a little every day can result in you achieving your dreams.

This is a book and a workbook - a book to provide guidance, information, and instruction; a workbook to access your financial situation and change behavior. You won't be as successful if you just read this book. Do the exercises and use them as a catalyst to help you reach your financial goals.

FOCUS ON THE FINISH LINE

Do you remember the story of the tortoise and the hare? Throughout the race between the two contestants, the hare would run ahead of the tortoise, stop to take a break, and then start again when the tortoise passed him. Throughout the journey the hare would tease the tortoise because he was traveling slowly, but steadily. In the meantime, the tortoise remained focused on his goal...the finish line. He didn't overexert himself, start and stop along the journey; he didn't become distracted by the antics of the hare. Slowly, steadily, and methodically he made the journey. Do you remember who crossed the finish line first? It was the tortoise!!

Why am I telling you this story? Because along your journey to financial freedom there will be scams and schemes that will appear to help you reach your financial goals faster. There will be enticements

4

along the way like fancy cars, clothes, homes, business ventures, get rich quick schemes, etc. that, if not properly analyzed and planned, can derail you from achieving your dreams. All of life's riches are available to you....in due time. Before you can splurge, you must master the basics. Doing so will ensure your financial success lasts a lifetime.

Which would you rather have, one million dollars given to you in one month or one penny doubled everyday for 30 days? This is not a trick question. If you answered one million dollars then you lose out because one penny doubled everyday would total over five million dollars at the end of 30 days. See the calculations below (*Table 2-1*).

A PENNY DOUBLED EVERYDAY FOR 30 DAYS

DAY	1	2	3	4	5
$$$	$ 0.01	$ 0.02	$ 0.04	$ 0.08	$ 0.16

DAY	6	7	8	9	10
$$$	$ 0.32	$ 0.64	$ 1.28	$ 2.56	$ 5.12

DAY	11	12	13	14	15
$$$	$ 10.24	$ 20.48	$ 41.96	$ 81.92	$ 164.00

DAY	16	17	18	19	20
$$$	$ 328.00	$ 655.00	$ 1,311.00	$ 2,622.00	$ 5,244.00

DAY	21	22	23	24	25
$$$	$ 10,488.00	$ 20,976.00	$ 41,952.00	$ 83,904.00	$ 167,808.00

DAY	26	27	28	29	30
$$$	$ 335,616.00	$ 671,232.00	$ 1,342,464.00	$ 2,684,928.00	$ 5,369,856.00

Table 2-1

This simple question is an example of how people want quick and instant gratification vs. waiting for the best rewards. It's a concrete example of **Proverbs 13:11b** that says, *"he who gathers money little by little makes it grow"* and the principle that compounding creates wealth. To become wealthy you don't have to come from a rich family, wealth can be achieved through discipline and investing.

Let's go back to my initial question. If you had chosen to take the one million dollars, did you have a plan for how you would use the money? Did you dream of paying bills off, buying a car, a home, or taking that long-awaited vacation? Did you have plans to invest some of it? If so, where would you invest it and how much of it would you invest? If you don't have answers to all of these questions, then you're like most people who receive a lump sum of money.

Did you know that most of the people who receive lump sum payments from lawsuits or lotteries end up back where they were financially in less then five years? Do you know why? Because most don't have a plan and the money gets squandered or swindled from them. It's like being the hare in our story. They get distracted by the pleasures and forget the goal of the race...make it to the finish line successfully.

Making and keeping money requires discipline, BUT discipline is not enough! You need a plan and you need to review your plan regularly. Advertisers and marketers invent things to get you to spend money. It's easy to get enticed to buy the hottest stock market trend, outfit, or techno gizmo; but getting enticed is what makes the marketers rich and you remain poor. That's why having discipline and a plan are so important. If you're not focused you'll plow all of your money into the latest hot trend, only to see it fizzle later along with all of your wealth.

Throughout the book I'll share tidbits with you up front because I've been there. I've made the same mistakes and now I know better. Even when you read this book, you'll probably make some mistakes of your own. But, if you come back and stick to the principles I teach, you'll be financially successful. Even better, over time you'll become a millionaire, *if that's your goal*, change your life and your family's forever. These principles will not be glamorous, sexy or fancy, BUT they have been used over time and have proven to work.

Remember throughout your journey, be the tortoise. Slowly and steadily, little by little, make it grow. The four principles that are the foundation of building wealth are **compounding, discipline, time, and save/invest automatically**. If you follow these principles, it's easy to build wealth and keep it. Let's get started.

COUNT THE COST

Go to the ant, sluggard; consider her ways and be wise; who having no guide, overseer, or ruler, provides her food in the summer and gathers her food in the harvest. - Proverbs 6:6-8

Have you been shocked at tax time when you realize just how much money you made? Have you ever thought about how much money, like water, passes through your hands over your working lifetime? The Social Security Administration sends you a Social Security Wage Compensation document every year, a few months before your birthday, so that you can verify that you've received credit for all income earned. This is also a great product for you to take inventory of how much you've earned compared to how much you've saved and invested.

Before taking a journey, it's best to map your trip from where you currently are to your destination. Getting from debt to financially prosperity is no different. To start your journey, let's take a financial snapshot of where you are currently.

TAKE INVENTORY

Here are a few exercises I'd like you to do. Please do at least a few of them.

Exercise: Take your annual Social Security report and add up all the amounts under the "Your Taxed Medicare Earnings" column. (Did you know that your Social Security is not taxed after earnings reach $97,500 however, Medicare is taxed against all of your earned income?) $_____ Were you shocked at how much you've earned?

Exercise: Go through your closet and calculate/estimate how much money you've spent on the items in it. $_____

Exercise: If you have a hobby like boating, shopping, sports, buying CDs, DVDs, video games, etc., calculate how much money you spent over the last three months. $_____

Exercise: If you hang with the guys or girlfriends drinking and clubbing, or if you smoke, calculate how much you've spent over the past six months. $_____

Exercise: Calculate how much you've spent on impulse purchases over the past six months on things like, fast food restaurants, clothes, entertainment, etc. $_____

Were you surprised at the amount you spent? If you did more than one of these exercises, did it answer part of your question, "Where has all of my money gone?" Was it easy to do the calculations or did you have a difficult time remembering what you spent over the past three to six months? Can you calculate how much you spent over the last month? $_____ Did you, like so many people, spend more than you make because credit cards make it so easy to say yes?

If you had difficulty doing this exercise I'd like to you track your spending for the next month. It's important that you do this because once you know how and where you're spending money, it will become easier to change your spending habits. Here are the steps I'd like you to take:

1) **Forget the past.** Don't beat yourself up over where you currently are. The past is the past, stop letting it rob you of your future and your blessings.

2) Use an envelope and put the receipts from everything you buy over the next month in the envelope. This way you don't have to keep a ledger or notebook.

3) At the end of the month, put the receipts in piles/categories according to what you purchased, e.g. food, clothing, gas, etc.

4) Add the categories.

I hope that this exercise helped you to determine where and how you're spending. Sometimes we spend money without giving it much thought. These few exercises should shed some light on how you arrived at the point of being in debt or using credit more often than you planned. Understanding how you got where you currently are will help you get out of where you currently are. Now it's up to you to decide whether you want to continue spending the way you do or make a change.

I wanted you to go through this exercise to see that when there is a lack of planning how you spend money, it can cost you your retirement, fulfilling your dreams, or your vacation. It may also keep you from getting that house you've always wanted or paying for your children's college education. It may cost you your peace of mind and so much more.

Planning boils down to forming a habit of budgeting and discipline. These two words may not be comfortable to hear, but is what you're doing now comfortable? Do you like the way things are going? In the next lessons I'll address budgeting and discipline, but first let's do a few more exercises.

Exercise: Calculate how much you make per hour. If you're an hourly wage earner, this will be very easy. If you're salaried, then take your annual salary and divide by 2,040 which is the average number of hours an individual works a year. What is your hourly wage rate? $_____

Keep in mind that your wage rate is before all of the taxes and deductions are taken; it's not your take- home rate.

Exercise: Calculate your average travel time to and from work and convert it to an hourly figure. _____ hours

Exercise: Think about the last large or unplanned purchase you made and calculate how many hours of work you invested for that purchase. _____ Do you feel your money and time were well spent? Yes/No

I asked you to do this exercise for two reasons. First, so that you can see that your time is money. Second, to show you that money is time, once spent it's gone.

CAN YOU AFFORD IT?

It's not uncommon for individuals to buy things because they say to themselves, 'I work hard for my money, I deserve this', 'I promised myself that when I started making my own money, nobody was going to tell me no', 'as long as I can make the payments, I'm buying whatever I want'. Does this sound familiar? You may have said these words or something similar at one time or another. So, what's wrong with these statements?

What's wrong is the attitude behind the statements. Making these statements is an indication of immaturity and a lack of understanding of money management. Spending is not a matter of whether you can pay for a purchase or not. Advertisers play on your attitude/ emotions with catchy phrases and slogans like, 'I'm worth it', '...you deserve a break today', '...have it your way', etc. to get you to purchase their product. It's not just on television, look at how ads are written in magazines and newspapers. Look at how products are displayed in stores, listen to the teasers on the radio and infomercials. Advertisers study their market and they study you to know which words and colors to use, that stimulate your senses, to get you to but their product. This is why there are free offers, trial periods, free samples, flexible payment plans, etc.

Ask yourself, "Can I afford it?" I'm not asking you to consider whether or not you make enough money to buy an item. I'm asking you to ask yourself: 1) Do I *need* the item?, 2) What am I giving up to have this item *(e.g. paying off your home, a debt free vacation or college education, retirement)*?, 3) How long will this item last?, 4) Why am I *really* buying this item? Sometimes shopping/spending is not about the item, it's about the *feeling* you get from buying the item. There *is* a difference.

The decision is yours to invest money to produce future gains or to spend on today's consumables. The decision *is* yours. I just want you to make an informed decision before you spend money, and that you spend for the right reasons. ***Spend wisely.***

THE POWER OF COMPOUNDING

Spending wisely is an important step to financial success. Here's why. During the Take Inventory exercises if you noticed where you consistently spent $100 a month on unplanned expenses, that could have been invested instead, you would have spent as much as $54,000 over a 45-year working lifetime. At first glance, spending $5 on lunch, $1.25 at the soda machine, and $10 at the drive- through of your favorite fast food restaurant doesn't seem like a lot. But when these little purchases are added up, it's not just $1,200 a year ($100 x 12 months) spent, but $200,561.38 over a working lifetime if invested at 5%. So how can $100 a month become $200,561.38? It's the power of compounding.

Are you a millionaire living a pauper's life?

15

THE LESSONS OF BEN AND ARTHUR

I don't know when I first heard the story of Ben and Arthur. I know it was not taught in any of my classes at school; so I must have read about them in an investment magazine. Although I saw the chart showing the comparison of their financial investments, I still didn't know the significance of this comparison until a few years ago.

Ben and Arthur's story demonstrates the power of compounding, systematic investing, and discipline. The table comparing their journey to millionaire status was created by the Ibbotson Associates. You can find the table on the next page.

In the table, you'll notice that Ben started investing $2,000 a year at the age of 19 and continued to systematically invest $2,000 every year until the age of 26. That's a total of $16,000 for just eight years. At the age of 65 Ben had amassed $2,288,996. Arthur didn't start his investment program until the age of 27. He invested the same amount, $2,000 a year, at the same 12% interest rate, as Ben, but he invested until the age of 65. That's a total of $76,000 for 38 years. Look at the difference in their earnings. Ben amassed $2,288,996 but Arthur only accumulated $1,532,166. Why, because of the power of compounding and time. Look at Ben's account. He has more than 13 times the amount in his account when he stopped investing than when Arthur makes his first deposit of $2,000!

16

BEN AND ARTHUR: THE POWER OF COMPOUNDING

*Ben and Arthur - Both save at 12% - Both save $2,000 Per Year - Ben starts at age 19 and **stops** at age 26 - Arthur starts at age 27 and **stops** at age 65*

AGE	BEN INVESTS		ARTHUR INVESTS	
19	$2,000	$2,240	$0	$0
20	$2,000	$4,749	$0	$0
21	$2,000	$7,558	$0	$0
22	$2,000	$10,706	$0	$0
23	$2,000	$14,230	$0	$0
24	$2,000	$18,178	$0	$0
25	$2,000	$22,599	$0	$0
26	$2,000	$27,551	$0	$0
27	$0	$30,857	$2,000	$2,240
28	$0	$34,560	$2,000	$4,749
29	$0	$38,708	$2,000	$7,558
30	$0	$43,352	$2,000	$10,706
31	$0	$48,554	$2,000	$14,230
32	$0	$54,381	$2,000	$18,178
33	$0	$60,907	$2,000	$22,599
34	$0	$68,216	$2,000	$27,551
35	$0	$76,802	$2,000	$33,097
36	$0	$85,570	$2,000	$39,309
37	$0	$95,383	$2,000	$46,266
38	$0	$107,339	$2,000	$54,058
39	$0	$120,220	$2,000	$62,785
40	$0	$134,646	$2,000	$72,559
45	$0	$237,293	$2,000	$142,104
50	$0	$418,191	$2,000	$264,665
55	$0	$736,995	$2,000	$480,660
60	$0	$1,298,837	$2,000	$861,317
63	$0	$1,824,773	$2,000	$1,217,647
64	$0	$2,043,746	$2,000	$1,366,005
65	$0	**$2,288,996**	$2,000	**$1,532,166**

Table 4-1   *...and he never caught up!*

The younger the better, the more the faster – make it automatic.

The reason Ben earned so much more was because he had more compounding periods than Arthur. Time was on his side. You can do the same thing. I wondered, if Ben was disciplined enough to save for eight years, how much more would he earn if he saved until age 65 like Arthur? Bottom line, if you're accustomed to living without $2,000, or $167 a month, why not continue? So I did the calculation, Ben would have $4,232,592 at the age of 65 if he continued to invest $2,000 a year. WOW!!!! DOUBLE WOW!!! Ben would have earned $2,700,426 more than Arthur by the time they both reached 65.

Why am I spending so much time talking about Ben and Arthur? It's because most of us can save $83.33 a month and a working couple can double that amount and save $167 a month. Unfortunately, most of us don't, because we haven't been taught the power of compounding.

COMPOUNDING TO RICHES

Here's another example of how compounding is a mathematical explosion! If you invest $1,000 at 10% compounded annually, the first year you'll earn $100 on your investment. But if you add the $100 of earned interest to your $1,000 and invest all of it in the second year ($1,100) at the same 10% interest rate you'll earn $110 and your investment totals $1,210. You earn interest on your interest! This might not seem like much, but over time your earnings explode; much like the earlier example of one penny doubling every day for 30 days. If all you did was invest $1,000 that earns 10% every year for 47 years, your earnings would total $88,197.64, but, if you decide to add $1,000 each year for 47 years, you'll earn $1,047,369.82! You earn over a million dollars by adding an additional $1,000 a year or $83.33 more per month. Here are charts that show the interest and savings (*Table 4-2 & Table 4-3*).

Growth of $1,000 over 47 years earning a 10% annual interest rate

YEAR	ADDITIONS	INTEREST	BALANCE
START	$1,000		$1,000
1	$0.00	$100.00	$1,100.00
2	$0.00	$110.00	$1,210.00
5	$0.00	$146.41	$1,610.51
10	$0.00	$235.80	$2,593.75
15	$0.00	$379.75	$4,177.26
20	$0.00	$611.59	$6,727.52
30	$0.00	$1,586.31	$17,449.44
40	$0.00	$4,114.48	$45,259.33
45	$0.00	$6,626.42	$72,890.61
46	$0.00	$7,289.06	$80,179.67
47	$0.00	$8,017.97	$88,197.64

Table 4-2

Growth of $1,000 over 47 years, $1,000 added annually, earning a 10% annual interest rate

YEAR	ADDITIONS	INTEREST	BALANCE
START	$1,000		$1,000
1	$1,000.00	$200.00	$2,200.00
2	$1,000.00	$320.00	$3,520.00
5	$1,000.00	$756.92	$8,326.12
10	$1,000.00	$1,829.54	$20,124.91
15	$1,000.00	$3,557.00	$39,126.98
20	$1,000.00	$6,339.09	$69,730.01
30	$1,000.00	$18,035.71	$198,392.83
40	$1,000.00	$48,373.73	$532,111.06
45	$1,000.00	$78,516.89	$863,685.80
46	$1,000.00	$86,468.58	$951,154.38
47	$1,000.00	$95,215.44	$1,047,369.82

Table 4-3

Do you see why it doesn't take a lot of money to become a millionaire? It is easier than you think. I heard a famous financial talk show host say, 'If it were easy to be rich, everyone would be rich'. Well, I've just shown you how it is easier to be rich than most of us realize. One of the keys to reaching your financial goals is to determine how much you'd like to accumulate, then have money automatically deducted from your pay each month to finance your investment. If you invest automatically, or as some say, "pay yourself first," you'll achieve your goals.

Wealth is achieved when you control money—money does not control you.

What prevents most individuals from reaching their financial security is lack of knowledge and lack of discipline; a **lack of knowledge** about how money works and a **lack of discipline** to develop a plan and stick to it.

I've just shown you how compounding makes a phenomenal difference in your earning power. There are two components to compounding that are critical for you to understand: first, the number of compound periods and second, the interest rate.

Here's why. The more compound periods, the quicker your money grows. It's quite simple: if you multiply your interest four times a year instead of once, your money will grow faster. Likewise, if you receive 20% interest instead of 10% you won't earn two times as much, your earnings will grow exponentially. I know I'm taking you back to some of your old algebra lessons, but hang with me while I give you an example (*Table 4-4*).

EXAMPLE OF GROWTH OF $1000 AT DIFFERENT INTEREST RATES AND ANNUAL COMPOUNDING

YEAR	AMOUNT	10%	TOTAL	VS.	20%	TOTAL
1	$1,000	$100	$1,100		$200	$1,200
2	$1,100	$110	$1,210		$240	$1,440
3	$1,210	$121	$1,331		$288	$1,728
4	$1,331	$133	$1,464		$346	$2,074
5	$1,464	$147	$1,611		$414	$2,488

Table 4-4

See the difference? At the end of year five, your $1,000 investment at 10% has grown to $1,611, BUT at 20% interest, it grew to $2,488. That more than doubles the original investment of $1,000. Now let's compound the periods quarterly instead of annually (see *Table 4-5*).

EXAMPLE OF GROWTH OF $1000 AT DIFFERENT INTEREST RATES AND QUARTERLY COMPOUNDING

YEAR	AMOUNT	10%	TOTAL	VS.	20%	TOTAL
1	$1,000	$104	$1,104		$216	$1,216
2	$1,104	$114	$1,218		$261	$1,477
3	$1,218	$127	$1,345		$319	$1,796
4	$1,345	$140	$1,485		$390	$2,186
5	$1,485	$154	$1,639		$467	$2,653

Table 4-5

Compounding works in your favor when you are the lender, who's investing, saving, etc. On the flip side, compounding works to your detriment when you are the borrower for credit cards, loans, etc. Earlier, I showed you two examples of how most Americans can become millionaires, one using Ben and Arthur who systematically invested $2,000 a year, ($167 dollars a month) that earned 12% compound interest, and another example using $1,000 a year at 10%, over a working lifetime. Not only can you become a millionaire, but also you can change your family history and legacy. It's a sad fact that most Americans will retire living on less than they made during their working lifetimes. Many will rely heavily on Social

Security or part-time jobs to fill in their retirement income gaps. Unfortunately, history has shown that many Americans will spend most of their retirement years scrimping to make ends meet.

BE DIFFERENT

You don't have to be like most Americans. Let's revisit the Take Inventory lesson and see where you have $100 or even $167 available each month. How much did you calculate you spend a month eating out, for your cups of coffee, shopping or other fancies? If you're like most people, a $5 cup of coffee at work amounts to $100 a month ($5 X 20 workdays = $100), if you smoke a pack of cigarettes at day $120 ($4 x 30 = 120), and a typical lunch out is $100 ($5 x 20 workdays = $100).

Your habit can be costing you your financial future. Is it worth it? If you see yourself in any of my examples, then you **can** be wealthy. You can also build wealth without making major changes in some areas of your lifestyle. I remember an applicable example that happened one morning at work. We have a breakfast club group at work. Every morning around 9 a.m. they make a trip to the coffee bar. Some buy coffee and a doughnut, others by orange juice and a breakfast sandwich. This particular morning, one of the bosses saw them return to the office with their goodies as he was filling his coffee pot with water. He commented on how much money they were wasting. Specifically he said, "I can get eight cups of coffee each day for the price you paid for just one. In fact, with the money you spend in one week I can buy a bag of coffee that lasts me a month. What a waste!" They just shrugged their shoulders and still continue to make their daily breakfast club runs. His statement is true. You can have your coffee and your millions too, just change how you acquire the coffee!

The government has a program to help you become a millionaire.

The government has established programs to help taxpayers retire wealthy but many do not take advantage of these tax breaks. I'm talking about Individual Retirement Arrangements (IRA), the 401 (k), and other tax exempt or tax deferred investment accounts. What's worse is some employers match a portion of the amount deposited in these investment instruments but workers don't max out the employers match. The employers' match is a guaranteed return on the investments…isn't that crazy?! I hope I'm not talking about you when I say these things. Let me give you an example of how your $167 a month can grow over the course of five years with an employer match of 3% (*Table 4-4*).

EXAMPLE OF $1000 INVESTED ANNUALLY AT 10% WITH EMPLOYER 3% MATCH

YEAR	AMOUNT	10%	TOTAL	3% MATCH	TOTAL
1	$1,000	$100	$1,100	$133	$1,133
2	$2,100	$310	$2,310	$246	$2,379
3	$3,310	$331	$3,641	$371	$3,750
4	$4,641	$464	$5,105	$478	$5,258
5	$6,105	$611	$6,716	$629	$6,917

Table 4-6

If you doubted your ability to become a millionaire, I hope your eyes have been opened and you see the possibilities. If you thought you had to have a lot of money to become wealthy or financially independent, I hope I've shown you that that's not true.

When I finally understood the power of compounding, I started paying more attention to my savings and investing. Unfortunately, I had some bumps along the way to my riches, and you may, too, but you can make it. Don't get discouraged. Stay disciplined, stay focused just like the tortoise, and you'll be rich.

Do you know Miss Oseola McCarty? Probably not, but you may know her story. Miss McCarty, was a washerwoman for about 73 years. She lived a simple life and saved her earnings. She probably didn't earn more than $12,000 a year. Yet, at the age of 87, she gave her life savings of $150,000 to the University of Southern Mississippi in 1995 to start a scholarship program. If Miss McCarty can amass $150,000 from her earnings, so can you and then some.

In 2008 the salaries of middle-income family was $38,000 to $60,000. There are no excuses for you or anyone else who works living a pauper's life. The old saying, "don't judge a book by its cover" is very true when it comes to how individuals manage money. I'm sure you're aware of lots of individuals who drive luxury cars, wear designer clothes, live in large estate homes with more rooms than family members, but are a pay check away from being broke. Why? Because they try to impress others by their lifestyle, while in reality they are living in distress. My stylist says, "People are just perpetratin" She's right. Many people want it now!! They ask the question "how much per month" instead of "how much". They charge it rather than of pay cash. You don't have to pretend. If you discipline yourself to save or invest just 10% of your take home pay, you will live a life of financial prosperity. You don't have to be a math wizard to figure out how much you need to save/invest either. Use any of the easy on-line investment or saving calculators to do the math. I've included some of them in the Worksheets section at the end of the book. You have no excuses.

You can be a middle-income millionaire!!!

GET A GRIP ON YOUR SPENDING

We've taken a snapshot of where you're spending your hard-earned money and looked at the benefits of changing your spending habits to save or invest. We've seen how compounding and automatic savings create wealth. So how do you take that knowledge and make it work for you? The first step to achieving wealth is to control spending through budgeting.

PLAN YOUR SPENDING

Most people live on a budget without even realizing it. Before they get their paycheck, they have already calculated in their head how much money they will get, what bills need to be paid, and how much money will be left over. A budget is the same except it's on paper and it's a roadmap for the future. Yet, the first image many people have when it comes to budgeting is a noose or handcuffs that restrict freedom…their freedom to spend. A budget or spend plan is just the opposite. The spend plan provides you with freedom and a guide to achieve your financial goals and objectives.

I've been turned off by overly complicated budgets. You know the ones that have five to twenty pages? Numbers have to be transferred from one set of spreadsheets to the other and every time you spend money, you have to record it on four or five ledgers. Maybe I'm exaggerating, but not by much. I've found the best budgets are the ones that are simple and quick to put together and track.

I've used a one-page budget for over 20 years and have had success sharing it with others. I want to share this budget with you as well.

Goals: "If you don't know where you're going, any road will get you there."
- Lewis Carroll

SET FINANCIAL GOALS

The other step to achieve wealth is to set goals. Why are goals important? I've found that when you have a financial goal, you become more disciplined with your money to achieve them; you're less likely to bust your budget.

Let me share an example. I remember assisting a woman who complained about being short every month, and sometimes she was behind in paying her bills. When we sat down to look at where she was spending her money, I showed her how she could pay off several bills using her next paycheck. She disagreed with me that the money should be spent to pay off bills because she had promised her son that she'd purchase the tuxedo for his prom, buy the couple's dinner, and contribute to the limo rental cost to get them to the prom! To me the prom was not as important as getting the bills paid, but it was to her. Fulfilling her promise or reaching that "goal" was the most important use of her money at that time. She was willing to make sacrifices to achieve her goal. I'm sure you've seen it too.

You probably know people who have gone on a retreat or vacation, bought outfits, booked their flight, hotel room, and wined and dined using credit cards. Because they used credit, they returned home to a pile of bills and were further in debt.

Maybe you know people who must get their hair done every other week, their nails manicured or buy a new outfit every month; maybe those individuals purchase stacks of CDs, *not the bank certificate of deposit*, and DVDs, buy the latest flat screen television or sound system, X-box 360, four-wheeler, eat out every week, etc, etc, etc,. You get the picture. All the while, they are renting their home and their furniture, maybe even their computer and leasing their car. They have nothing in savings and even less in their expensive looking wallet or purse.

I share these examples to make a point. If we decide it's important enough to have, we find a way to get it!! Setting goals is a driving force to get what we want.

Without a plan, it's just a dream!

WHO'S GETTING RICH?

Our habits and consumer buying power can make other people rich. Do you remember when having a boom box was the bomb? If we want it, a market will be created to give it to us. Here are some examples to demonstrate what I mean.

The African American hair market is a multi-billion dollar industry. Yes, I said *billion*. If you want your hair black, blonde, purple, or green, straight, wavy, curly, short, long, or cropped, you can have it; and "it" doesn't have to be your own hair if you buy it. As braids, weaves, cornrows, waves, and texturizers became more popular, more and more vendors entered the market. As African Americans changed their hair styles, products were designed to accommodate them: pressing irons, flat irons, crimpers, curlers, twists, wigs, hair pieces, extensions, hair for braids, any color any style, real, synthetic, curly and straight. If it was needed, it was invented. Beauty supply stores popped up in every neighborhood. Getting to them is convenient; you don't have to have a car because stores are so numerous. They're in the neighborhood shopping center which is within walking distance.

Another industry that has taken off is nail salons. Fifteen years ago the nail salon business was limited to the manicurist in beauty salons or spas. Today, they are a community staple. This repeat business has grown exponentially. Bi-weekly visits to get nails polished, manicures and pedicures, cost $20 - $40 a visit; fillings and artwork can cost as much as $10 per finger. This growing business generated an industry earning over $6 *billion* in 2008 according to National Public Radio.

What does this mean for you the customer? If you visit a salon on a bi-weekly basis as recommended, the cost is usually $30 per visit or $60 a month. It's important to look your best; however, that same $60 invested at 5% can generate a return of $9,345 in 10 years. The point I want to make is Every Penny Counts. It's important to balance what you need with what is "nice to have". You might ask why I used a low rate of 5%. Well, 5% is a reasonable rate of earnings on a certificate of deposit, a U.S. inflation adjusted or corporate bond. Although getting a 5% interest rate does not generate a lot of earnings, I hope you see that every little bit helps you get closer to your financial goal. Bottom line, instead of $60 a month going out of your household every month for 10 years, you investeded it and received $9,345 into your household in 10 years.

These are just a few examples of new consumer markets. There are others like IPods, blackberries, cell phones, tattoos, designer clothes/ handbags, oversized pants and shirts, designer sneakers, electronic games, etc. These markets are designed to stimulate the economy and that's a good thing. However, when splurging in the market results in personal financial crises, we have to tell ourselves, and sometimes our family members, **NO** and budget accordingly.

GO ON A DIET

Sometimes we have to go on a spending diet. Have you every done that? I have. I remember when I used to sew a lot I would constantly go to the fabric stores. Just like some people shop until the drop in department stores, I shopped in fabric stores. Every time I went into one, I came out with a bundle of fabric and patterns determined to make something new. But life would happen; I'd get busy with work, the children, and other commitments so the fabric just piled up. One day when we were moving, I was shocked at how much fabric I had accumulated; some still had the price tags on. I was so appalled that I put myself on a one-year diet from buying fabric. You may think this was easy, but it wasn't. I was addicted!!! BUT, I did it!

At the end of the one-year diet I had gotten fat...fat in my purse that is. I saved over $1000 by not buying fabric! I learned a lot about myself during that year. I learned I was stronger than I thought. I learned how to manage my emotions better; I was able to go into a fabric store and look around without buying. I also learned that I could use that same kind of control in other areas of my life.

Since going on the fabric buying diet, I've put myself on other diets like "no new clothes for a year", "no new shoes for six months", and others. I know old habits are hard to break; but getting control of your spending is a necessity. If you see yourself in my story, start by putting yourself on a diet for a week or a month. Taking little steps will help you complete your journey. If you're really serious and want more out of your money, say to yourself "enough is enough". Try the "no _____ (you fill in the blank) diet for a _____ (fill in the time period)". It's worth it.

YOU HAVE THE POWER

In 2006 the 38.3 million African Americans had a buying power of $744 *billion*. They spent most of their money on the three C's – cars, clothes, consumer goods such as electronics, and less than most of the U.S. population on the A-B-Cs – **A**: assets like homes and businesses, **B**: books/education, and **C**: creating wealth through investing.

Did you know that women make 80% of the buying decisions for their families? The amount of money women control is debated. Some studies state that by 2010 women will control more than half of private U.S. wealth, or about $14 trillion. A <u>Business Week</u> and

Gallup study state the amount will be 60% of the country's wealth. I'm sure you'll agree with me, that either of these figures represent a lot of money and buying power. Isn't it important that if women have access to and control over such large sums of money it should be managed well? Planning, budgeting, and goal setting is key.

Adults aren't the only group affecting the marketplace. The U.S. Census Bureau reports that the 25.3 million teens, between the ages of 13-18, have an average annual income of $8,130, (from allowance, gifts, and part-time work). Their parents contribute $5,496 of that amount. Teen buying power is $216.3 billion annually. Why am I giving you these numbers? Because the Bureau also reported that, the money teens spend is pure disposable income. In many cases teens had more disposable income than their parents!

Here's something to think about. I've shown you that investing just $2000 a year can result in millions of dollars at retirement. If parents can contribute $5,496 a year towards their children's disposable income, why can't they invest some of the money for their retirement and wealth building? Isn't there something wrong with this picture?

I've given you several examples of how you may be contributing to other peoples' wealth. Unfortunately, of the billions of dollars spent on things, most of it is spent to purchase consumable items, things that are disposed of or useless in 2 to 3 years or sooner if the fad or trend goes away. If this describes you and you want to be wealthy, this has to change. When you set goals, it's easier to stick with a budget to achieve them. What are your one, three, and five year financial goals? Write them here so that you can refer to them as we build your budget.

FINANCIAL GOALS: _____

_____

_____

_____

_____

_____

_____

Now that you have your goals written down, let's get to the heart of budgeting. As I said earlier, most people already have a budget of some form. You probably are like most people; you know how much you're being paid and how much you owe. In some cases, you may have money left over or you may not have enough. I'd like to show you a simple but powerful budget tool that I've used for over two decades. The great thing about this budget is 1) it's easy, 2) it's a monthly and an annual budget, and 3) it's automatic.

BUDGET IS NOT A BAD WORD

I want you to focus on the benefits of having a budget because it is the foundation to achieve financial success. Don't view the budget as a document that keeps you from spending money. There are *ONLY 3* steps to building the budget below; I'll walk you through each of them.

Let's consider the Robinson Family. Their budget on page 38. I've also included a copy of the Robinsons' budget at the back of this book and a blank form for you to use. (One of the keys to the budget is keep it to one page. To make it easier to work with, the blank form in the back of the book is presented on two separate pages. However, once you've fined tuned your working budget, reduce it back to one page like the Robinson's.) Tear both out and refer to them as we build your budget.

You'll notice the budget I designed accounts for the way we spend money every day. Look at the category "Entertainment" for example. In our sample budget, the Robinsons set aside $10 for in-home movies and $50 for eating out. When they engage in these activities, they have peace of mind knowing they can afford this luxury and don't have to worry that another bill won't get paid. You could include in your Entertainment category paint ball, golfing, judo or piano lessons, or whatever you want. It's all up to you. Then you decide how much money you want to spend for each activity each month. This is why the budget gives you freedom instead of restrictions. The beauty of this budget is you'll do the same for **every dollar** you plan to spend each month. This is your family's and your budget; you decide how much YOU WANT or PLAN to spend. When you develop your budget always round up the change and use whole dollars.

With this example (*Table 6-1*) as a backdrop, let's go through the process of setting up your entire budget. Look at the budget layout. The first line, or header, has a place for your annual salary, your name and the date you developed your budget. The date is important because as you fine-tune your budget you'll be able to track your progress. It's a great motivator. On the right side of the first line, annotate your monthly take- home pay. Include all of the money you have coming into your household each month. There are three parts to building your budget. First, **budget every penny.**

MARY AND JOHN ROBINSON'S BUDGET
As of 1 Jan 2009

Salary $70,816   Take Home $4,818

CATEGORIES	TOTAL	1ST	2ND	CATEGORY TOTAL
1. GIVING				
TITHE/OFFERING	330	165	165	
GIVING				330
2. HOUSING				
MORTGAGE	2000	1000	1000	
ELECTRIC	200	200	0	
CELL PHONES	160	0	160	
CABLE	100	100	0	
WATER*	32	0	32	
HOA	41	41	0	
SECURITY	41	0	41	
MAINTENANCE*	200	100	100	
				2774
3. FOOD	250	125	125	
				250
4. TRANSPORTATION				
PAYMENT	430	0	430	
GAS	160	80	80	
TAGS/INSPTS*	15	0	15	
INSURANCE*	30	0	30	
MAINTENANCE*	50	0	50	
				685
5. HEALTH				
MEDICAL CO-PAY	30	30	0	
DENTAL CO-PAY*	15	0	15	
DISABILITY	39	0	39	
LIFE INSURANCE	39	0	39	
				123
TOTAL				4162

CATEGORIES	TOTAL	1ST	2ND	CATEGORY TOTAL
6. CLOTHING				
PURCHASES*	20	10	10	
DRY CLEANING	6	0	6	
				26
7. ENTERTAINMENT				
MOVIES	10	5	5	
EATING AT WORK	50	25	25	
				60
8. RECREATION				
VACATIONS*	200	100	100	
JUDO LESSONS	60	30	30	
				260
9. MISCELLANEOUS				
SALON/HAIR CUTS	80	40	40	
				80
10. ALLOWANCE				
ADULTS	50	25	25	
				50
11. SUBSCRIPTION				
NEWSPAPER	15	15	0	
				15
12. GIFTS*	50	25	25	
				50
13. INVESTMENTS				
SAVINGS	50	25	25	
401(k)	0	0	0	
RETIREMENT	0	0	0	
				50
14. DEBTS	BALANCE	MINIMUM PAY		
MACY'S	200	15	0	
CAPITAL ONE	1000	50	0	
				65
			$56	4818

*Variable Expenses $612   FirstFruits Ministry © 1982

Table 6-1

This isn't overkill by any means, it helps you account for where you spend your money and it's your safety net that funds are going exactly where you want them to, to improve your quality of life. We want to ensure we have a zero balanced budget. That's a budget term that simply means when you add up the amount you spend each month on paper, the total is equal to the amount you bring home each month; there's nothing left over. Second, **plan and then spend**. Do you remember the saying, "if you want to know a man's priorities, look at his checkbook?" I don't quite agree with that saying because sometimes money is spent because of lack of discipline instead of misplaced priorities. Third, **allocate which paycheck or funding source you'll use**.

THE BUDGET SET-UP 1-2-3

The basics of how the budget is set up is 1) left to right, 2) need to nice, and 3) whole, then part. Let me explain.

Step 1. Left to right.

Look again at the Robinsons' budget. On the **left side** of the budget are all of the must have items. These are your fixed costs. This includes things like housing expenses, e.g. mortgage/rent, electricity, water, gas, phone service, insurance, etc., and auto expenses, e.g. payments, gas, repairs, parking, inspections and tags, and food/groceries, health or medical expenses. What should be included on the left side of your budget are the necessities you must have each month. If you pay for braces, childcare, homeowners association dues, security alarm monitoring, and lawn service, these go on the left side. On the **right side** are the nice to haves/pleasantries of life or variable expenses. This includes clothes, yes clothes, entertainment, recreation, vacations, hair care, subscriptions, gifts, allowance, and other niceties.

The budget is set up this way to ensure your life necessities are funded before you spend money on anything else. Doing so guarantees you don't have to worry about the lights getting turned off or not having enough money for gas and food if you go on a shopping spree to take advantage of the latest sale. I'm sure this makes sense to you, but I see people buy clothes, dine out, and take vacations, even pay on their charge bills, while at the same time they are late or delinquent on their mortgage and utilities. That's crazy!!! This budget will help stop these practices.

Let me clarify a point before I go further. I don't have anything against buying clothes, vacations, or gifts, nor do I have an issue with taking advantage of sales and charging things. The key to financial success is having a plan. Money is set aside for these expenses before the purchase occurs. Using this type of budget ensures when the charge bill comes you are able to pay it in full because the cost of the item was ALREADY included in your budget.

Step 2: Need to Nice

This part of the budget refers to the categories you use to build your budget. Some people ask what category should go first, second, third, and so on. It's strictly up to you. Look at the categories the Robinsons used for their "needs" on the left side. They included giving, housing, food, transportation, and health. Notice that some of their "nice" categories on the right side include clothing, entertainment, recreation, and allowance. As a believer, my first category is designated for giving my FirstFruits, i.e. my tithes and offerings. If Uncle Sam can get his take before me and everybody else, then surely I want to give back to God before I pay anybody else; including myself. (May I get on my soap box for a few minutes? I believe God's word that I rob Him when I don't give my tithe. I believe as I am obedient to His word, God takes my trust in Him and my obedience and makes the 90% left over go further than the 100% if I had kept it. You may not agree, but I challenge you to try it for 2-3 months and see for yourself.)

For most people the "need" categories would include housing, transportation, food, day care, health, and insurance, then, the "nice" categories would include clothes, entertainment, vacations, and investments. I hope you get the picture. You can have as many categories as you like, BUT, the budget that people stick with are simple and easy to maintain. As much as possible, limit your budget to one page.

Step 3: Whole then part.

In this step, you determine how much you will spend on each item in your budget, this represents the whole. Then determine which paycheck you'll use to pay the expense. This represents the part. You'll see in the Robinsons' budget that they include a column labeled first and second because they get paid every two weeks. The columns are labeled to represent how much they will allocate from their first paycheck and then the second paycheck each month for each bill. If you get paid every week, then you'll have four columns. However, if you pay bills twice a month, you could simplify your budget and make two columns to match when you pay bills. Like I've said, this is your budget and it's important to design it to fit your personality and the way that works best for you.

Let's walk through an example using the Robinsons' budget for Housing. It's listed on the left because it's a need; notice that mortgage is first because it's their most important need. They have budgeted $2,000 per month for their mortgage but pay bi-weekly $1000 from each paycheck. If you look at their cell phone, they pay $160 a month but pay the bill using their second pay check. This is the process for each category and every item in the categories. Quite easy don't you think?

Look at the right side of the budget. This side is for the quality of lifestyle or variable expenses. It's up to you what you want to include. Let's talk about the gifts category. Included in this category are all of the gifts you expect to purchase throughout the year. I know you don't have a crystal ball, but some gifts are known. These might include, Christmas, birthday, anniversary, Mother's and Father's Day, things like that. You might have a friend or relative who's getting married or graduating from school; include these gifts in this category also. You get the picture? Once again, the goal is to capture all of the expenses you'll incur for the year and break it down to a monthly amount.

Now is also a good time for me to explain the concept of the Allowance category. It's a designated amount that you can spend without giving accountability or tracking. Since all the major expenses are budgeted; e.g. salon, clothing, food, transportation, etc., this category is synonymous with pocket change. It has no strings attached and can be used for small unforeseen spending like a going away luncheon, contribution towards flowers for a sick co-worker, a spontaneous get-together with friends, a stress massage visit, etc. The Allowance should be kept to a small/ reasonable amount because all other expenses are budgeted. I hope you get the picture.

Let me take the time right here to answer some what-if questions you might be thinking about.

BUT, WHAT IF...?

Question: What if you don't pay a bill every month, because it's cyclical – quarterly or annual payments. This would include expenses such as homeowners association dues, auto insurance or tags. What do you do?

Answer. The budget is designed to put your spending on auto pilot. To do that, all of your expenses are broken down into a monthly amount. If you have a bill that only comes quarterly, divide the quarterly expense by three and that amount is entered on your budget. For example, if your car insurance payment is $90 a quarter, divided by three (90/3) gives you $30 per month. On your budget you'll enter $30 so that when the bill is due you'll have $90 available to pay it. It doesn't matter if you enter the $30 in the first or second paycheck column, as long as your monthly take-home balances to zero.

Let's look at another irregular expense like Vacation. The Robinson's plan to spend $2,400 on their annual vacation. Therefore, they take that total $2,400 annual amount and divide it by 12 to get a monthly figure. Each month they set aside $100 from each paycheck so that when they go on vacation they spend the money they've saved throughout the year. It's a lot like having a vacation or Christmas club account at your local bank, but this way you're accounting for it in your monthly budget.

Question: What do you do with the money that is set aside for cyclical expenses?

Answer: You automatically deposit it in a high interest bearing account so that it's available when you need it. The cyclical expenses like vacation and gifts are denoted with an asterisk* by the expense title. Calculate the total of all expenses that have an asterisk and divide it by two. (Annotate the total of cyclical expenses at the bottom of your budget.) Each pay period, automatically deposit this amount in the high interest bearing account.

In the Robinsons' budget, their cyclical expense total was $612. They divided $612 by two to get $306 each pay period. The $306 is automatically deposited in an interest bearing account, the same place they put their emergency money, to be used when the bill or expense arrives.

There are two benefits gained from using this strategy. First, the money is available when the expense occurs. Second, it's also a quick way to increase your emergency fund. This is a buffer if an emergency arises that exceeds your current emergency fund savings. If this happens, naturally adjust the variable expenses that can be delayed. For example, the Robinsons could spend less on their vacation, postpone it, or cancel it altogether to cover an unforeseen expense if their emergency fund balance was not sufficient.

Question: What about future expenses that I don't know when they will occur or how much it's going to cost, like major car or house repairs?

Answer: For these expenses, estimate what the average bill would cost. For example, if your home is 25 years old, consider when the roof or appliances should be replaced. Research to find out how much it could cost and how soon the replacement would occur. Take that amount and divide it by the amount of time you have until the expense arrives. ($24,000 roof repair to occur in 48 months requires a set aside of $500 each month.) Notice the amount the Robinsons set aside for house maintenance. They plan to make some major renovations to their home in three years. By setting aside $200 per month for three years, they'll reach their goal and will not have to borrow against the equity in their home.

The dollars for these future expenses is also asterisked and the money deposited in your interest bearing account until the expense comes. You'll see the account balance grow quickly over the course of the year. I want to warn you, don't lose focus on your goal and forget why the money is being saved. If you get the urge and spend it on something else, you'll create a financial crisis for yourself and your family in the future.

As you develop your budget, as much as possible, account for every expense that will occur in the calendar year. We want to make the budget simple to track and easy to use. Once all of the things of life are broken down to a dollar value and these values represent the lifestyle you want to live, then the imaginary budget handcuffs or straightjacket come off.

WRITE YOUR BUDGET

I hope I answered most of your questions. Let's get back to setting up your budget. When determining your expenses for utilities, food, gas for your car, etc., it's usually best to start by using the higher monthly amount you've consistently paid throughout the year. This will allow wiggle room in your budget if the bill is routinely lower than you budgeted. However, don't use an amount that's too high, this will create unnecessary padding in your budget. This usually leads to waste or losing track of where money really is being spent. It takes about three months to get a realistic working budget. As you continue to modify the budget, update your spreadsheet until you have one that works. That's the importance of the date at the top of your budget.

I've told you how and why the budget is set up the way it is. Now, let's build your personalized budget. Make copies of the blank form at the worksheet section of the book so that you'll have opportunities to refine your budget as you go through the steps. Don't be concerned about your budget balancing out to your take home pay for now. We'll resolve that in a few steps. Set up your categories based on what's important to you and the order in which your bills come. Don't try to change the way your mind works to fit the budget, make your budget fit the way you see things. By this I mean, if you want to include lunch under food instead of entertainment, by all means do so. If you want to include dining out in this category also, you can, but I would not recommend it. The reason why I wouldn't is because dining out is not a necessity. Also, it's an area where you can spend a lot of money without realizing it.

By the way, including dining out in the food category is another one of my pet peeves. It's easy to blow your food budget with dining out. A drive-by to your favorite or convenient fast food burger or pizza place can cost hundreds of dollars each month. Whether it's at work, a busy day out with the children, or you're tired and don't want to cook, dining out can cost you more than you'd planned. Before I get off my soapbox, allow me to share an experience. I was helping a young lady set up a budget to see where her money was going; her goal was to become debt free in 12 months. I suggested she record every time she spent money or keep the receipts in an envelope because she used her debit or credit card most of the time. She was shocked to learn that she was spending an average $25 per day in her dining out category. How? She routinely bought coffee and a pastry at the office deli, then she'd have a mid-day snack, lunch, and a drink; and all of this was at work. Then if she worked late, she'd get a take-out from a local restaurant. Her $150 monthly dining out budget actually was more like $500 a month; and to make matters worse, she also had been buying groceries!!!! This is why I recommend entertainment, specifically, dining out be kept on the right side of your budget where "nice to have" expenses are budgeted.

I know this was a lengthy example, but I hope you see how the budget should be tailored to fit your priorities and how it can be used to bring some expenses under control.

Fail to **Plan** = **Plan** to Fail

BALANCE THE NUMBERS

If you're like most of the people I assist with budgeting and getting out of debt, when you wrote your first budget using this technique, you spent on paper more money than you bring home. For many, this is an ah-ha moment. If that's the case with you, let me explain why. For the first time, you've accounted for how your life really does work; you can really see how much money you're spending, and realized that the reason you're broke at the end of each pay check is because life happens.

I remember helping a friend with her budget, the numbers she told me to use to create her budget reflected she had $150 to $300 left over each paycheck, but she was always struggling. When we wrote her budget using this template, she realized that she had not accounted for her insulin, bi-weekly hair and nail salon visits, her quarterly doctor visits, and annual eye and dental exams. She also had not accounted for her monthly $100 dry cleaning bill. Also, she was planning to go to her family reunion and had not considered the airfare, hotel, and food costs. You may have encountered the same things when you put your life on paper and equated it to financial numbers. So what's next?

Life is made of choices. You must decide what's most important. If you were able to zero balance your spending to you take home, congratulations. But, if you spent more on paper than your take home pay, now you must decide what you should cut back on so that your budget balances. Here are some of the most common areas where you can cut back: 1) eating out, 2) buying clothes, 3) vacations – take shorter ones or less expensive ones, 4) personal services such as dry cleaning, hair and nail treatments, 5) gifts, and 6) reduce cable, cell phone, and internet services to the necessities. (I usually recommend this even if your budget is balanced. Who really uses three movie channels, two sports channels, and a DVR at the same time? How many ring tones and other services are you paying for on your cell phone each month?) If these steps resulted in a zero balance on paper, congratulations!

But, what if your budget didn't balance because you owe more than you make? Here are some suggestions: 1) Cut back and cut off some of the nice to have items. 2) If you get a sizeable IRS refund each year, then you may be struggling because you've reduced your take home pay too much. Let me explain. If you receive a tax refund of say $5,000 from year to year, then you're cutting your take home pay short by $600 a month, ($5,000/12 = $600). Work with a member of your Finance or Human Resources Office to determine how much you should raise your personal deductions so that you receive more in your take home pay. I don't recommend you cut to the bare bones so that you owe each year, but don't give the government an interest-free loan at your expense either. 3) Generate extra income. This may include some overtime, a part-time job, or getting a much deserved and needed raise, 4) Delay some purchases, and 5) Shuffle some of your expenses to a later time in the year. Let me expand on recommendation number 5.

SHUFFLE SOME EXPENSES

If you get paid every two weeks, then you essentially receive two extra bonus checks a year; usually in May and October. Since this budget takes into consideration what you bring home each month, it accounts for spending two paychecks a month. The two extra checks you receive may be used to pay for annual expenses; e.g. gifts, annual medical check-ups, vacations, and clothing purchases. By shuffling these expenses to come out of your two extra paychecks, (maybe even four if you're married), then you can eliminate that expense from your budget.

Take these steps when you shuffle expenses. First, determine the take home amount of these extra pay checks that you'll have available. Second, deposit that amount in your interest bearing account, DON'T TOUCH IT! Third, delete the expense from your budget. Finally, fourth, withdraw the money when the budgeted expense arrives. Notice I said "budgeted expense". The same principle applies for these expenses as in your monthly budget... plan on paper and then spend. I recommend you use this same methodology anytime you receive a windfall check, this includes a bonus, refunds, and cash gifts; deposit the money in an interest bearing account and plan how the money will be spent. If you don't, you probably won't remember what you did with the money.

EXECUTE YOUR BUDGET

Now that you have refined your budget on paper, it's time to execute it. Using this budget shifts your focus from living payday to payday to living on a monthly income. The first couple of months may be a little challenging because you're accustomed to focusing on paydays. Hang with me as I explain the process.

1) Deposit your paycheck into your financial institution.

2) The money for cyclical expenses should be set up to automatically transfer to a high interest bearing account.

3) If you prefer to use cash to purchase food, gas, and your allowance, cash a check for these expenses each payday and annotate the withdrawn amount from your checkbook balance. Pay for these expenses using the cash you've withdrawn. If you prefer instead to use a debit or credit card, or even write checks to pay for these expenses, you can. Just be sure to annotate the expenditure in your check register.

4) Pay your monthly bills as usual and annotate the payments in your register. Don't spend more than you budgeted on paper.

5) Note that the amount of your actual bills may not equal the amount you budgeted. If you budgeted correctly, you should have enough allocated of each expense without a lot of excess. Leave the excess in your bank account so that it's available when bills fluctuate like utility bills. If the excess amount becomes substantial, transfer this money to your high interest account. However, if the excesses occur often, you have allocated too much toward an expense and you should rebalance your budget.

6) Put your budget on autopilot. You no longer have to focus on paydays using this budget strategy because money has been delegated for each bill and now it's available. There should be no surprises or gotchas. The only time you make changes or adjustments to your budget is when there is a change in your income or your bills.

Now you can have financial peace and no longer worry about having money to pay your bills. I hope this shows you the power of budgeting and planning.

Come out of bondage…plan to become debt free.

GET DEBT FREE

Changing your behavior toward money and sticking with a budget could be a major lifestyle change…but it's worth it. If you're tired of owing people, borrowing from Peter to pay Paul, and living a life of lack, having a budget will change your life for the better. I guarantee it.

Once you begin to plan first, then spend, you'll eventually owe fewer people. Once you save and then buy, you'll have more money because you'll **earn interest** rather than **pay it**. Even though the amount you earn won't be as much as the amount you would have paid, the fact that you're not paying interest is a lot like making it. Do you understand what I'm trying to say?

Here's what I mean. Suppose you go to your local retail store and purchase the latest flat screen television for $500 on credit at 18% interest. The salesman asks you how much you want your monthly payments to be and you agree to pay $50 a month. Here's something most of us don't do, we don't look at the loan papers to see the final cost of that $500 television, the other costs that are tacked on, or any unnecessary insurance or warrantees they convince buyers to take. The $50 a month 18% loan comes to a total cost of $550 over 11 months. However, if you'd saved $50 a month and earned 5% interest over the same period of time you would amass $600. Then you could pay cash for the television and keep the extra $100 of savings. Because you have cash, you might be able to negotiate an even better price. Discipline is the key. If you can discipline yourself to pay $50 a month to pay a debt, then you can discipline yourself to save $50 a month. I hope this example shows you how making these kinds of changes over time helps you become debt free. Don't fall victim to answering the questions "How much per month?" or "How much do you want to pay?" Instead, you ask the question, "What is the total cost?" There is a big difference when you ask, "What is the TOTAL cost?". I hope you see that in the example above.

FIRED UP AND FOCUSED

What if you already have a lot of debt, how do you become debt free? I'm glad you asked. Before you get out of debt you have to have a made up mind to do so. You have to become fired up and focused to do everything to get out of debt. This includes making all the sacrifices necessary to get there. Once you get focused, there are six steps in our budget plan to help you become debt free. Look at the debts the Robinsons have as I walk you through the steps.

Step 1: Stop accumulating new debts; cut up credit cards. Buy essential items only and only those included in your budget. Notice I said essential items not "need" items. The difference is some of the items included in your "need" budget possibly can be cut back until you become debt free. Your lifestyle may change during this period but it will be worth it. Also, most people can become debt free within 2 to 3 years when they are fired up and focused. I tell my students, if you had enough money to get in debt, then that also means you have enough to get out of debt; it's up to you how long it will take.

Why do I say this? Loan and credit card companies extend credit based on your income and your ability to pay. Being overwhelmed in debt occurs when individuals take on more debt than they can manage and then begin a cycle of taking from one source, like taking equity out of their home, to pay another. When that cycle is broken, you get traction and begin to make progress and become debt free.

Step 2: List all of your debts from the smallest to the largest balance. We're not going to focus on the interest rates because our goal is to pay off as many debts as possible in the quickest amount of time.

Step 3: Add the lender and the minimum amount on the right side of your budget. Label the category "Debt". But, include the payment to your monthly "need" to pay total. This means you must reduce the amount available from the "nice" to have total to balance your budget. (NOTE: Placing debts on the right side is an exception to our rule. The reason they are placed here is that the goal is to pay them off. Usually, debts arise because the expense was not factored into your monthly spending, which now they will be.) You're probably already doing this step in your head each month, but now you're putting it on paper and have a concrete plan on how the debts will be paid. Also, you know when they'll be paid off.

Step 4: Look at your budget and determine expenses that can be reduced or eliminated, for a period of time, so that you can pay your debts off faster. These funds are added to the minimum balance of the smallest bill until it's paid off. Continue to pay the minimum on all remaining debts.

Step 5: As each bill is paid off, the freed up money is added to the next bill so that it is paid off faster. Like dominoes falling, you'll begin to pick up speed. The minimum continues to be paid on all of the other bills. Here's an example of what I'm talking about. Take a look at the Robinsons' Spending Tracker (*Table 6-2*).

The Robinsons owe $200 to Macy's but only have to pay the minimum of $15 a month. In order to pay the bill off quicker, they have decided to reduce their vacation fund to $100 and use the other

MARY AND JOHN ROBINSON'S SPENDING TRACKER
As of 1 Jan 2009

CATEGORIES	TOTAL	JAN	FEB	MAR	APR	MAY	JUN	JUL	AUG	SEP	OCT	NOV	DEC
1. GIVING													
TITHE/OFFERING	330												
GIVING													
2. HOUSING													
MORTGAGE	2000												
ELECTRIC	200												
CELL PHONES	160												
CABLE	100												
WATER*	32												
HOA	41												
SECURITY	41												
MISCELLANEOUS*	200												
3. FOOD	250												
4. AUTOMOBILES													
PAYMENT	430												
GAS	160												
TAGS/INSPTS*	14												
INSURANCE*	30												
MAINTENANCE*	50												
5. HEALTH													
MEDICAL CO-PAY	30												
DENTAL CO-PAY*	15												
DISABILITY	39												
LIFE INSURANCE	39												
6. CLOTHING													
PURCHASES*	20												
DRY CLEANING	7												
7. ENTERTAINMENT													
MISS	10												
EATING AT WORK	50												
8. RECREATION													
VACATIONS*	200	100	100	100	100	100	100	100	200	200	200	200	200
JUDO LESSONS	60												
9. MISCELLANEOUS													
SALON/HAIR CUTS	80												
10. ALLOWANCE													
ADULTS	50												
11. SUBSCRIPTION													
NEWSPAPER	15												
12. GIFTS*	50												
13. INVESTMENTS													
SAVINGS	50												
401(k)	0												
RETIREMENT	0												
14. DEBTS													
MACY'S	15	115	85	0	0	0	0	0	0	0	0	0	0
CAPITAL ONE	50	50	80	165	165	165	165	165	0	0	0	0	0
TOTAL	4818												

FirstFruits Ministry © 1982

Table 6-2

$100 to pay more toward their debts. Currently they spend $65 per month towards debt reduction. By adding an additional $100, they have $165 to put towards paying off their debts. As a result, they will be able to pay off their Macy's bill in two months. In January, they'll pay $115 against the $200 balance and in February they'll pay off the remaining $85 balance. Also, in February, they'll add $80 towards their Capitol One bill ($165-$115 = $80). In March, they'll pay $165 on their Capitol One bill and will continue to do so until the balance is paid off in September. After September, they'll be debt free and will be able to increase their vacation fund back to $200 a month. In addition, they will also have $65 to use for other expenses or savings. The Robinsons' revised Spending Tracker shows how they paid off their debt. I've included in the worksheet section an example of a more expanded version of a Debt Reduction Plan that has multiple debts and how to structure a debt reduction plan. There's also a blank form to use if you need it.

As you build your debt reduction plan follow the same guidelines that the Robinsons used. But don't stop there. If you're really fired up and focused to become debt free look for other sources of revenue to apply to your debt. I've seen individuals generate money from garage sales, returning items back to the vendor, selling jewelry, taking on part-time jobs, and cutting back to bare bones.

Cutting back to the bare bones does not automatically equate to living in poverty. I remember when our family was growing faster than our paychecks I used tactics to stay within our budget but still maintain a good quality of life; I still use some of them today. For example: 1) I didn't shop for food until I had a menu. To stretch our dollars I'd buy ground beef in large quantities so that I could prepare spaghetti, sloppy joes, lasagna, meatloaf, and hamburgers throughout the month. The more trips to the grocery store you make the more you spend; shop one to two times a month. 2) I purchased full size or family size packages because individual servings are more expensive. Chips, cookies, fruit treats, etc. were purchased this way and later separated into individual snack baggies for our children. 3) We had low-cost entertainment every Friday. Our family "camp outs" included a rented movie, frozen pizza, and popcorn. The children would put their blankets on the family room floor, eat pizza and popcorn, watch movies and fall asleep in the late evening hours. 4) We took "daycations" before they became popular. I took a map and drew a circle the distance of 50 miles from our home address. On the weekends we'd take trips within that circle so that our family had opportunities to take mini vacations. These were a lot of fun and inexpensive because we'd have breakfast at home before leaving, I packed a picnic lunch and we were home by bedtime. Our only expense was gas. I share these memories with you because I want to show you that cutting back doesn't have to result in a dull or boring life. You can become debt free by looking at ways to save money, ways to generate other income, and being fired up and focused.

BUDGET BUSTERS

Look at your spending habits to find things that cause you to get off track. I call these "budget busters". Budget busters are things that can blow your budget out of whack and keep you from becoming debt free. Budget busters happen when you have an unexpected car or home repair. It could develop when there is a medical bill or even utilities are higher than expected. To minimize budget busters, set aside $500 to $1000 in a high yield money market deposit account before you begin to focus on getting out of debt. This emergency fund will buffet unexpected blows and keep you from having to shuffle money by robbing Peter to pay Paul or using credit cards to pay for emergencies. Also, the money you set aside for the cyclical expenses you identified when you built your budget will be added to your emergency fund. These funds will provide an added cushion and some flexibility if your emergency account is not fully funded at the time you need the money. Replenish all money withdrawn from the emergency fund quickly.

If you have difficulty identifying resources to put in your emergency fund, try holding a garage sale, consign items, work overtime and/or part-time, put off the usual Christmas and vacations, use extra/ bonus paychecks and refunds, cut eating out, buying clothes, and other recreation. Bottom line, if you're committed to becoming debt free you'll find the resources and you will not regret the sacrifices. Finally, don't go it alone. Get your family involved. Educate your family on money management. Set goals together and you will break the family's debt legacy.

SPENDING TRACKER

Now you can shift your focus to your spend plan. Track how you're spending money and measure it against what you "planned" to spend. The Spending Tracker is an excellent tool to chart your monthly spending to ensure you stay within your budget. Reign in spending so that it doesn't derail your opportunity to accomplish your financial goals. It is also your roadmap for planning the next year's budget because you'll record actual spending throughout the year. Look again at the Robinsons' Spending Tracker to see how it is arranged. Your budget totals are in column one so that you know how much you've budget for each category; then the months are placed across the column headings so that you can record your actual expenditures. As I've said with the budget, it's important to keep everything simple. After seeing everything on paper, most of the people I've worked with tightened their belts and were debt free in two to three years. A blank Spending Tracker form is also included in the worksheet section of this book (*see page 126*). I know you can become wealthy using this plan. Many have and you don't have to be the exception.

DROWNING IN DEBT

What if you've cut to the bare bones and you still can't make ends meet because you owe too much to too many people. If this is the case, here are steps to get you through.

Step 1:   Contact your lender, not the Customer Service attendant. I don't have anything against them, but many are not in a position to negotiate alternative payment plans. If they are, then work with them; if not, ask for a manager in the debt resolution department.

Step 2: Be honest and up front with your lender that you've tried everything to repay them.

Step 3: Discus your financial situation and the steps you've taken to repay your debt. Speak from a position of strength and professionalism, **don't whine.** Tell/show them your budget and your debt reduction plan. Focus on the facts. Don't accuse or get angry.

Step 4: Negotiate a *written* payment or settlement plan. These could include:

a. A reduced lump sum payment to cancel the debt in full. Ensure the amount forgiven will not have tax consequences.

b. Suspend future interest rate accruals on the debt and no future charges. In some cases this agreement also entails canceling the card.

c. Reduced or lower interest rate.

d. Stop fees, e.g. overdraft, late payment, annual, insufficient funds, etc.

e. Pay an agreed amount monthly over an agreed time to pay debt in full; e.g. $60 for 60 months.

Step 5: Maintain contact with the lender to let them know how you're progressing. Stick with your agreement. If you have problems keeping your arrangement, let your lender know. Don't hide the truth.

These steps won't change your credit history but they will provide you with a game plan and reduce some of your stress. If the debt goes to a collection agency, work with them. Some may get pushy and aggressive, but don't accept harassing telephone calls, threats, or contact with your employer or family members; that's against the law.

I encourage you to stay focused and don't give up, no matter where you are in this process. Be the tortoise, focus on the finish line. Others have overcome and become financially successful. You can too!

We've covered all the steps to building your budget and tracking your expenses; pretty simple right? It takes about three months to fine-tune your budget so that you're capturing all of your expenses. Remain focused throughout this budget building process because it's going to reap great dividends and payoffs for you and your family.

Once the budget is fine-tuned, you don't have to adjust it until there are changes in your expenses or your income. That's why everyone with whom I've used this template, likes it so much. You'll know which bills are coming in, when the payment is due, and which paycheck you'll use to make the payment. Your monthly spending is now on autopilot. Your unplanned spending is limited to your allowance only because everything else is accounted for; haircuts, clothes, food, mortgage, etc. In addition, your long-term and cyclical expenses are funded because you set aside money every month toward the total cost. You don't have to worry about any "gotchas" when the bill comes in.

DON'T GET RIPPED OFF!!!

*Through wisdom a house is built, and by understanding it is established;
and by knowledge the rooms shall be filled with all
precious and pleasant riches. - Proverbs 24:3-4*

Companies are determined to get as much of your money as possible. A recent marketing report revealed the buying power of 39 million African Americans will reach $1.1 trillion dollars by 2012 and earlier I shared that some studies predict that the buying power of women will reach **$14** trillion by 2010. More importantly, these market researchers show an increase in purchases of luxury items like cruises, cars, designer clothes, and consumable goods. It's OK to buy these goods if you can truly afford them. Unfortunately, many people stretch themselves so thin in the wallet that they **appear to be** affluent instead of **really being** affluent. By this I mean many use any financing method available to get the "things in life" that they want now.

Here's what I mean. I was visiting family in Miami, FL just before the Super Bowl game and the television airwaves were filled with advertisements from rent to own and electronic stores encouraging people to buy a big screen television to watch the game in style. They had many gimmicks like "90 days same as cash", "only $99 dollars down and $100 a month", "no interest until 2012" and "no payments until 2012 next day delivery". The parking lots were filled with people buying televisions...most of whom could not afford them. I'll talk about these finance options more in depth later in the book, but I want to share why these types of impulse buys are tantamount to financial suicide.

Same as cash, no money down, and deferred payment plans include large interest payments, usually in the high double to triple digits. The reason is quite simple. If you owned an appliance or furniture store and gave your customers the goods without paying, how long would you be in business? What would you charge in return for trusting them with your merchandise? Before you answer, consider that after a year the furniture, carpet, or appliance will be used and worn. It would no longer be in mint condition. Consider that if the item were returned due to payment default, how much money would you be able to make from it when you resell the item. With this in mind, if you were the store owner, would you sell the item for the price it costs with a little profit added in? Probably not, right? Well, neither does the company that plans to stay in business. So how do they make up for the risk they take? The answer is they jack up the price. The storeowners charge more interest than what is considered reasonable. That's what happens with these types of deals. A big screen television that sells for $2,200 on a two-year same as cash deal would result in a final cost of $3,271.22. That's $1,271.22 in interest.

These types of sales tactics are becoming more prevalent and successful because people want it "now," and also because many believe they will pay the item off within the "same as cash" or "no interest" time period. The truth is, 70%-80% of buyers don't pay the loan off during the no-interest period and end up paying penalties, and interest is calculated back to the date of purchase.

There are so many scams, shams, and outright rip-offs like these that are perpetuated to get your hard-earned money. Every day people are devising ways to get money from you, some are legal, some border on illegal, some are outright scams, and some should be categorized as criminal.

No longer are there clear laws to protect the buyer. The old saying "let the buyer beware" is very true today. Usury, full disclosure, and truth in lending laws have been changed, watered down, and enforcement relaxed so much that you have to have the Wisdom of Solomon to avoid the traps.

Here are a few that I'll go more in depth on: credit cards, Rent-to-Own, Same as Cash, instant IRS rebates, Car Title Loans, Free Trial Offers, Credit Repair Companies, Debt Consolidation, Subprime loans, lotteries, and Instant Savings on store credit cards.. There are more out there such as cash a check, car and appliance warrantees, accidental death policies, life insurance on loans, and many, many more.

BUYER BEWARE!

I listed the above programs because many people use them without fully understanding them or their real cost. If used improperly they cost you lots of money. Advertisers have done a superb job because credit cards, payday loans, rent-to-own, same as cash, and instant IRS rebates are so well known in our society today that many people don't regard them as loan vehicles – but they are.

Did you know that if your credit card balance is $500 and your interest rate is 24%, if you never charge anything more and paid the minimum of $25 a month, it would take you 26 months to pay off your credit card? Paying the minimum would cost you an extra $134.35 in interest charges. Would you agree with me that this is ridiculous?

Did you know that because rent-to-own is considered a lease and not a purchase, there is no limit on how much interest the store can charge you? I bet you didn't know that most people who sign up for instant IRS rebate checks pay an excess of 100% annual interest on the loan. That is ludicrous!!!! Instant IRS cash rebates is considered an **anticipation loan**. The high interest rate that's charged for these loans should be outlawed. If the individual waited for a few weeks he/she would get 100% of their tax rebate interest free.

These are some of the things companies do just because the buyer doesn't have the knowledge. The lessons in this chapter will change that for you. We're going to break the silence and change lives and livelihoods. We're going to break the cycle of poverty and lack and move to a cycle of wealth and success.

CREDIT CARDS

Would you go to your bank, fill out an application for a loan, stand in line for approval, and wait for the teller to give you money for a meal at your favorite restaurant? Would you do it to purchase a pair of shoes or to purchase your favorite DVD? Would you do it to purchase gas? You probably answered NO!! It is ludicrous to do such a thing.

When you use a credit card, you're taking out a loan or better stated, using a line of credit issued to you from the bank. Your credit card limit is the maximum amount of your bank line of credit. When you applied for your credit card, you agreed to specific terms and conditions like, "repay in full within 26 days of receipt of the bill – the grace period – otherwise interest would be added". The convenience of not having to go to your bank, filling out an application for a loan, standing in line for approval, and waiting for the teller to give you your money often makes it easier for people to charge more on credit cards. Although a credit card is an empowering piece of plastic, a sign of "I've made it and I have money," it can be the death of financial dreams.

Do you remember a time when your grandparents and great-grandparents paid cash for everything? Did you ever wonder why? It's because credit cards, as we know them today, weren't around. Getting credit and taking out loans was considered a bad thing. They saved for almost everything they bought. Only big ticket items like homes and cars were purchased "over time". They may have run a tab at the local grocery store or supermarket, but the tab was very small and paid immediately the next payday.

Credit cards didn't arrive on the scene until 1950. The first credit card venture began with Mr. Francis McNamara in New York City. The card was used to pay for meals at restaurants, hotels and air fair, hence its name Diners Club. In 1951 Franklin National Bank of New York got a piece of the action by offering a card that could be used more widely. Seeing there was money to be made, Bank of America in San Francisco started their card, BankAmericard. Today this card is known as VISA. By 1958 American Express got into the game with their signature card.

Even with some of the big boys in the game, the card didn't get much action or acceptance until the end of 1960 when banks started sending cards to everyone who had a name and address, regardless of whether they asked for one or not – regardless of their credit standing. A card in everyone's pocket made it acceptable and helped it gain national acceptance. In 2008 over 1.5 billion, that's right billion, applications went out every three months to entice people to use credit cards. It worked!!!

Would you believe that in 2008 Americans charged over $968.4 billion on credit cards, and that number is going up almost seven percent each year? The average American owns eight credit cards and carries an average balance of over $8,000 each month according to the Federal Reserve Board. Worst of all, most make the minimum payment each month. Remember what I said previously about minimum payments? I don't think many people would willingly pay $10 or more for a hamburger, but many are paying that and more when they make minimum payment for the meal they charged at their local fast food or chain restaurant. Since credit cards have been accepted at fast food restaurants, a survey revealed that sales have risen 31%. During the survey individuals admitted that if they did not have a credit card, they would not have purchased a meal because they did not have cash on hand. Additionally, sales research has shown that since cards have been accepted, cardholders spend more. The average individual purchase increased by 30%.

Getting a share of the African American credit card business is also big business. It is estimated that Black households will spend over $980 billion dollars in credit card purchases in 2010.

I don't have anything against using credit cards. My concern is when credit cards are used improperly because of a lack of knowledge or lack of planning. I can't blame the card holder because banks use a lot of double speak in their advertising and on their applications, making it confusing to understand their terms and conditions. They do it on purpose. I doubt that some bank executives could clearly and accurately state their fees and interest rate calculations so that a fifth grader could understand them. I can't blame the banks either, because banks are in the business to make money…and they are good at it because they make lots of it. What I want to see is a level playing field. The banks can make as much money as they can as long as they clearly tell the cardholder the terms and conditions of using their card.

It's up to you to understand your credit card terminology – all cards are not the same. Read the back of the credit card application and the billing statement, ask questions if you don't understand. Not knowing will cost you money.

I'm going to try to simplify some of the key terms and rules for you. Before I do, let's do an exercise to test your working knowledge of your credit card. If you have a credit card, answer these questions?

Exercise 1: How is the interest due calculated?

_____

Exercise 2: When does your grace period start and end?

_____

Exercise 3: What is your annual interest rate? _____ What is your monthly interest rate? _____

I hope this exercise was easy. If it wasn't, read your credit card contract. Usually the terms are on the back of each monthly bill.

Believe it or not, according to a survey conducted by CreditCard. com, 75% of credit card holders surveyed stated they did not read the terms and conditions of their card lender. Do you suppose that's why many pay late fees and are charged unnecessary interest?

Don't let this happen to you. So, let's get started with some credit card terminology and lingo.

Interest rates or finance charges are stated as an Annual Percentage Rate (APR). The annual rate is divided by 12 to derive the monthly percentage rate. The rate is usually applied against your unpaid balance. If your card company has a 24% APR, for example, divide this rate by 12 which is the monthly rate you're charged ($24/12 = 2$) on your outstanding balance.

This may not seem like a lot of money, but in May 2009, banks reported they anticipated over $20 billion dollars in revenue from customers paying interest and late fees. Now you see why so many companies want to get into the credit card business? Not just banks, but department stores, gas companies, and even colleges want a piece of the action because most card holders don't pay their balance in full. Therefore most of the interest they receive is pure profit.

Once upon a time there was a limit on how much a credit card company could charge in interest. Before 1996, only a penalty fee that ranged from a flat $5 to $15 dollars was charged. But in a U.S. Supreme Court case of Smiley vs. Citibank, the courts lifted restrictions on the amount that can be charged for late payments.

After this ruling interest rates skyrocketed. You'll see more of what I mean when I talk about other types of loans and scams.

Let's look at some more credit card terms.

Annual or membership fee is the rate charged to use the credit card. Some cards have a FREE introductory fee the first year but then charge a fee starting the beginning of the second year. In addition, some cards are "no fee" but the company makes up the difference by charging a high interest rate or finance charge. Always remember, the lender is going to make their money.

Grace period is the time when interest in not added to new purchases. If your card has a 26-day grace period, you're not charged interest for 26 days from the date of purchase if your charge has not posted at the bank. But, if it's not paid, you will be charged interest. Also, any balance carried to the next month is charged interest immediately after the grace period ends. Most people don't realize that there is no grace period for cash advances. Interest is charged immediately and sometimes the interest rate is higher. I can't stress it enough: get knowledge, read the terms.

Late fees: Some companies charge a late fee if you're just one day late making payment or if the payment is posted one day after the due date. These fees could be as much as $29 and are in addition to interest rate charges.

Penalty fees and transaction charges are added on top of the interest rate. These penalties could be for cash advances, going over your credit limit, paying your bill late or paying with a check that bounces. If your bill goes up but you haven't charged anything, penalties and fees might be the reason. If your check bounces, don't be surprised if the lender processes it a second time and also charges a retroactive late fee.

Minimum Balance. This represents a portion of the amount due on your purchases. It can be as little as 2% to 2.5% of the outstanding balance. Remember, paying the minimum balance costs you money and makes money for the issuer. In 1980, one well-known company studied which credit card holder would generate the greatest amount of profits for their company. What they found were individuals routinely made minimum payments but kept a large balance were the most profitable. They targeted this clientele with low introductory rates that later were raised to excessive high interest rates on the unpaid balance; in just ten years the company earned more than $100 billion. Other card companies noticed and followed their lead.

Introductory or teaser rates are low rates charged for three to six months. Usually, introductory rates are used to get individuals to transfer or roll over their balance from high interest rate cards. Most times, balances are rolled over with the intent of paying off the transferred balance during the low rate period. Unfortunately, most often, the balance is not paid off and the interest rate is raised a lot higher than the previous card. To make matters worse, if spending is not controlled, then the unpaid balance can get higher than the transferred amount because spending behavior/habits haven't changed.

These are some of the more common terms associated with credit cards. Credit cards are big, big business for the lender and usually a win-win for them. Read the terms of your contract to level the playing field in your favor. Pay your balance off each month. If you preplan your purchases, have the cost included in your budget/spend plan, then it's easy and automatic.

I know I spent a lot of time on credit cards. This is because it's the most common and often used type of loan. It's also the most abused. Fortunately, credit card reform is on the way. In 2010 institutions will have to explain their terms and conditions more clearly. Also, they will be required to give advance notification of interest rate hikes. But don't be fooled that this reform will solve the problem.

Companies are already devising plans on how they will continue to keep their profits high. Some of the tactics being discussed include reducing or eliminating the grace period, charging higher fees, and reducing reward programs.

So how does telling you about credit cards and its pitfalls fit with the book title, "Every Penny Counts"? Let me share another example. If you charged $2,000 on your credit card, made no more purchases, and pay the minimum balance of $50 per month at 24% as required, how long will it take you to pay off the balance? Did you divide $50 into the $2,000 balance and came up with 40 months or three years and four months? If you did, your answer would be wrong. The reality is it would take you 82 months or six years and eight months to pay off the balance. That's a long time!!!! Furthermore, in addition to paying off the $2,000 balance, you also would have paid $2,064 in interest.

However, suppose you added $25 to your minimum payment? In other words, you paid $75 per month against that $2,000 balance. How long would it take to pay off the balance? Only 39 months; three years and three months!! That's right. While 39 months is still a long time, it's a lot shorter than the 82 months. Also, you only pay $887 in interest. By adding 25,000 pennies or $25 every month, you pay the bill off 43 months or three years and seven months faster and save yourself $1,177 in interest payments. I know you can come up with an extra $25 per month. I hope this example shows you why it's so difficult to pay off a credit card if you make charges and make minimum payments. It's nearly impossible to pay off a credit card while charging!

Before we leave the subject of credit cards here are some tips that will increase your financial success.

1) Carry one major credit card, e.g. VISA, American Express, MasterCard, Discover, etc. Most companies accept the major cards; therefore carrying several cards increases the chance you'll charge more. (Most Americans carry between five and 10 credit cards; don't be in this number.)

2) Say "no" to the special offers to save 10% with your purchase. The savings is good only for that purchase and usually carry a higher interest rate.

3) Pay off your balance in full. This means using your credit card for items already included in your budget. If your balance is not paid in full, store your card in a safe location that you can't easily reach and don't charge until your balance reaches zero.

4) Find a card with a low interest rate.

5) Don't charge more than 50% of your credit card limit;

if your limit is $3,000 don't carry more than a $1,500 outstanding balance.

PAYDAY LOANS

Payday loans are usually quick and easy to get because the lender is in the business to make money from excessive finance charges. To qualify for the payday loan a pay statement and a form of identification is all that is required. These loans are usually for small amounts, as little as $100 to $1,500. Women, military personnel, minorities, and individuals who make less than $25,000 a year are usually the target audience.

Technology has made these loans so easy to get. There are over 2.5 million internet links for payday loans, four million for cash advances (get cash immediately with the promise to pay later) and 31 million for check advances (hold the check until I get paid). Why so many? Because there are websites that teach individuals how to run a payday loan operation to earn money from the comfort of their homes. For as little as $300, kits can be purchased to help individuals set up their own business. The websites boast about earning 30% or more on every dollar and they teach tactics on how to get more from the customer, how to boost returns, and how basically to "scam" innocent people.

Payday loans are due in full the next payday and carry interest rates as high as 390 to 780 percent annually. It's not uncommon that a cycle of using these loans is created because of the high interest rates. In some cases the lender agrees to collect a portion of the loan and carry the note for the balance until the next pay period. In other cases the loan is rolled over to create a larger loan because interest is included. On average, an individual can have as many as 8 to 10 payday loans a year.

Many times the payday loan stores misrepresent themselves. They portray themselves as authorized check cashing establishments, when, in fact, many are not state regulated. I was visiting in a city and saw an advertisement that looked like a bank commercial. The elderly woman stated how helpful the two cashiers had been to her over the course of several years, they treated her like family and helped her through many tough financial times. The commercial was so slick that it wasn't until the end of the commercial that I realized the advertisement was for a payday loan store. As I drove throughout the city, payday and check cashing stores lined the main highways, but only on one side of town…the poorest.

Don't be fooled or become a victim of payday and check cashing loans. These stores don't provide a service, they prey on individuals who are financially struggling and usually make their financial situation worse.

Stay away from them. If you must borrow, use a bank, credit union, or even a family member. At least the rate you'll be charged, even if it's high, will be regulated.

CAR TITLE LOANS

These loans are a lot like the payday loans, the primary difference is that you offer your car title to get money. Car title loans/pawns are another fast growing business. The lenders usually give the individual a lot less than what the car is worth and the loan must be paid usually within a month. As a result, most individuals default or end up renewing their loan month after month for a higher amount. This usually results in the borrower eventually losing their car.

Title loan businesses usually charge 25% interest per month, which is a whopping 300% per year; and they add on fees. Just like the payday loan tactics, rates can get in the three-digits, up to 600%, because most states don't have an interest rate cap. Car title loans are a trap. Don't become a victim to their slick television adds. These businesses are called predatory lenders because they prey on people that can least afford it.

I can't say it enough, if you need to borrow money, use a bank, credit union, or even a friend or family member. At least the rate you'll be charged, even if it's high, will be regulated.

RENT-TO-OWN

You might ask why I included Rent-to-Own in this chapter. The reason is because many states have allowed these businesses to market themselves as providers of rental services as opposed to providers of loans. But, in fact, they, too, are predatory lenders. Let me explain.

I spoke earlier of the television advertisements for the Super Bowl. Some of them were Rent-to-Own places. They promised a television in your home with payments as little at $10 a week for 78 weeks. Since many people can afford a $10 payment, they think nothing of the real cost of owning the television. The real cost of the payments comes to an annual interest rate of 220% and interest and finance charges of $560. The bad part about this scenario is that the buyer could buy the television out right for as little as $200 if they had saved and paid cash.

Rent-to-own is a multi-billion dollar business. They are in the sales business, not the rental business. They sell appliances, furniture, televisions, computers, and jewelry, payable on a weekly or monthly basis. The reason they can get away with calling themselves a rental business is because back in the 70's they convinced most states to declare their services as a lease-based and not a purchase-based enterprise.

Predatory lenders have the same agenda: take as much of your money as possible. They don't provide a service, they have worked the laws in their favor to keep you broke and themselves rich, and they prey on individuals that are usually struggling financially.

My message to you: save money and pay cash. If you have the discipline to pay someone $10 a week, then you have the same discipline to save $10 a week. You'll come out ahead every time.

SAME AS CASH – NOTHING DOWN

This sales tactic is everywhere; cars, appliances, furniture, carpet, computers, and tools. In most cases of same as cash deals, the lender has already raised the item's price to cover expenses. Once the purchase is made, the company you bought your item from sells your sales contract to a finance company at a profit.

Here's how the finance company makes their money and why they are willing to buy your contract. Most purchases (70% to 80%) made under the "same as cash" program are not paid off during the "no interest" period. If the money isn't paid in full at the end of the same as cash term (usually one to two years), the finance company charges all of the back interest, from the date of the purchase, to include penalties. That's why these programs are classified as an "interest deferral loan". These important terms are written in the fine print of the contract.

When the loan is not paid, the interest rate charged is much higher than if you took out a regular contract to pay for the item over time. To make matters worse, the finance companies tack on expensive life and disability insurance, this is pure profit for them. The bottom line is to save, pay cash or make a purchase contract; either way you'll save money in the long run.

INSTANT IRS REBATES

Patience is the key when it comes to getting your income tax check back. Instant IRS Rebate checks is another growing business that is a predatory lending scam. When these types of loans first surfaced, only the income tax preparers used them. Now car dealers, appliance and furniture stores, and others are in the game. Why? Because there's lots of money to be made.

Instant tax rebates are classified as an "anticipation loan"....on your own money. The way these loans work is the lender determines how much you will receive in your tax refund and agrees to advance the money to you. The problem with this is the interest rate charged for you to use your money is usually in excess of 100%. The IRS reported in 2007 that nearly 12 million taxpayers paid over $1.9 billion in loan fees to get their refunds faster. These fees raised the real interest rate paid on the loan to as much as 700%. In most cases, borrowers received their loan money only one to two weeks faster than if they had waited for their refund directly from the IRS.

Instant tax refunds are targeted to individuals who make $35,000 or less a year. Many don't have bank accounts, and are encouraged to get their refund now because their refund can be put on a pre-paid debit card. Don't pay interest on your own money. Wait and get 100% of what's due to you.

FREE TRIAL OFFERS

You've heard the saying, "if it sounds too good to be true, usually it is". Consider this saying anytime you hear radio and television advertisers who offer you a free trial. Usually these free offers come with a hidden price tag. The first price tag is usually the shipping cost. When you make the telephone call, this is how the sales pitch usually goes. The telephone receptionist says the item is free but you have to pay the shipping and handling costs to receive it. Then they explain there is a limited time period in which to try the item. If you are not fully satisfied you can return it. However, if the item is not returned, you will be charged. That's the second price tag. Therefore, they need your credit card number. Also, if shipping is free, you'll have to pay, on the other hand, when you return the item; that's the third price tag.

The popular free trial offers include monitoring, like your credit report or identify theft protection and automatic replacements, such as supplements, diet foods, and skin care products. Once the company receives your credit card information, they automatically bill your credit card every month. The companies that offer monitoring are betting that you, like the majority of their clients, will forget when the free trial period is over and you won't cancel the program before the monthly charges begin. Most people go for a year or more before they realize they've paid for the monitoring services. The companies that offer automatic replacements ship the goods and you, the purchaser, begin to stockpile items until you run out of storage space...usually five to six months later. In the meantime, the companies are getting richer and richer because you accepted their FREE OFFER. If the items were really free, the company would not be in business. If the company wasn't making money from the advertisements, you wouldn't hear about them. FREE TRIAL OFFERS is a BIG and PROFITABLE BUSINESS. If you really are interested in trying a free offer, annotate on your calendar when the trial period expires. This will remind you to cancel the service if you don't like the product. Also, be sure to read the fine print to ensure you have not agreed to a specific trial period, that you must return unused products, or pay shipping charges. Also be mindful that anytime you allow a company to have access to your banking information you have given them some control of your finances; companies have been known to withdraw outstanding balances from banking accounts without the owner's approval.

CREDIT REPAIR COMPANIES

The airways are also filled with companies that promise to help you clean your credit and repair your credit score. Many of them charge an upfront fee, ask you not to contact the credit reporting agencies, fail to discuss your consumer rights, and promise you they can get rid of negative information on your credit report even though it's correct. These companies are scams. The Federal Trade Commission (FTC) states that they have never seen a legitimate credit reporting agency that makes these claims. It takes time to clean up bad credit. There is no quick fix. Depending on the type of consumer debt, information remains on your report seven to ten years if it's correct. You have the right to contact the credit reporting agency if there is incorrect information on your report and they are required by law to make the correction within 30 days free of charge. Don't fall for credit reporting company schemes and scams.

DEBT CONSOLIDATION

Taking all of your bills and rolling them into one payment seems like a great deal, however, it has drawbacks. Before considering a consolidation loan, examine the interest rates of all of the bills you want to consolidate and compare those rates to the consolidation rate. In many instances, it's not uncommon for individuals to roll lower interest rates or low balances into a rate that's higher. This increases your cost of the original loan. Also ensure the over-spending habit has been resolved. It's not unusual for individuals to return to the pre-debt amount before the consolidation loan is paid off. Before entering into a consolidation, ensure the pay-off period is less than the sum of the individual bills. By this I mean keep your new monthly payment as close to the total monthly payments of the original loans without going over. The fact that there is only one payment instead of several creates a false sense of financial soundness.

For example, if you have six loans with interest rates that range from 12% to 24%, insure your new interest rate is as close to the 12% rate as possible. Also, if the total monthly payment on the six loans is $600, then keep your new payment as close to $600 as possible. This will reduce the total pay-off period and avoids the temptation to take on more debt.

Items that depreciate in value, like cars, credit card debt, and vacation loans, are usually the types of bills that are rolled into a home refinance, or money is taken out to pay these bills off. Be cautious of rolling these and other debts into a home refinance. Why? Consider this: Does it make sense to pay for a car or a vacation for 30 years?

By this I mean, in your effort to consolidate your bills into a 30-year low interest home refinance, you'll pay for the consolidation loan over the period of the refinance. I know lenders pitch the benefit of consolidating debt into a mortgage refinance because the interest can be written off on your tax return. That's a pitch that should be called a fowl. The result is the new mortgage becomes higher than the existing mortgage balance, therefore the benefit of getting a reduced interest rate may be lost when you roll in a debt consolidation. This also means paying more interest over the life of the consolidated amount than you probably would have had on the original loan. If you choose a debt consolidation loan consider getting a stand-alone loan the interest rate will be higher but the payoff will be shorter and your home will not be at risk.

SUBPRIME RATE LOANS

Do you know your Fair Isaac Corporation (FICO) score? In the 1960s, the Fair Isaac Corporation came up with a scoring mechanism that rated the risk a lender would incur when making a loan. The higher your score, the more likely the creditor would receive their money; the lower the score, the greater the lender's risk. Lenders charge a high interest rate on lower FICO scores because they assume a greater risk. Now this seems backwards to me, why charge a higher rate to the person that cannot repay. That puts more stress on the borrower and increases the probability they won't repay. However, that's not how the lending industry looks at things.

The difference between the rates charged for a high and a low FICO score can be as much as 1.5% in interest. Depending on the loan amount, this could be thousands of dollars a year. For example, on their website, FICO gives an example of a 30-year home loan for $150,000. If the FICO score is 760-850, the interest rate was 4.95 and monthly mortgage payment of $801, but a score of 620-639 results in an interest rate of 6.54% and a mortgage payment of $952 a month. That's a big difference!! The individual with the higher FICO would save over $9,500 a year. FICO scores are used for mortgage and car loans, credit cards rates, and even employment qualification. To improve your FICO score it's important that loans are paid on time and paid off quickly.

But don't be fooled. Just because you have a high FICO score does not always guarantee you'll receive a low interest rate. A study conducted in 2002 revealed that middle income African Americans were three times more likely to be charged a higher interest rate than whites were even though they qualified for a lower rate. Also, lower income individuals were two times more likely to be charged a higher rate. Even worse, lower income whites with a low FICO score were charged a rate lower than middle to upper income

African Americans with high scores. What this means is African Americans paid more than their white counterparts. The Wall Street Journal reported in 2006 that 61 percent of all borrowers receiving subprime mortgages had credit scores high enough to qualify for prime conventional loans. In 2009, these percentages were up even more.

The key to getting a lower rate is to be current in your debt payments, shop around, and be aware that businesses with finance or mortgage in their name are more likely to charge a higher rate. This includes car dealerships, appliance financing, and mortgage companies. Shop around and do an apples to apples comparison. This is why the annual percentage rate (APR) is so important. Remember, once you sign the note, the bill is yours; protect your financial interests at all times and ask "what's the total cost not monthly payments".

LOTTERY

Today it's easy to be tempted to gamble. Lotteries began in the early 1800s but grew exponentially since the 1980s. Forty-three states, the District of Columbia, Puerto Rico and the U.S. Virgin Island had legalized lotteries in 2008. Whether a mega million, scratch off, Power Ball, Mega Ball, pick 3, 5, or 7, or the Fantasy 5, the probability of winning lotteries is astronomically low. For example, the probability of winning the U.S. power ball is 1 in 80,089,128, and winning the New York lottery is 1 in 18,009,460. The odds are always purposely stacked against the gambler. A Tax Foundation study revealed in 2005 that over $52 billion, yes billion, was spent to play lotteries. It revealed that lower-income households, those making $20,000 - $29,000, spent more playing the lotteries than wealthy households did. It also revealed that Blacks with a high school diploma or less education spent more per month playing lotteries than any other race or educational level; the average spent was more than $67 per month. Did you know that if the same $67 a month was invested at 5% for five years compounded quarterly, the amount saved would be $10,436. At the end of 45 years, the average working time, the amount saved would be $135,488; that's more than most people have saved at retirement. Playing the lottery is a losing proposition every time. Why do I say this? Because 75% of the individuals who have won large amounts playing the lottery were broke within five years of receiving their winnings. In most cases, they were worse off financially because they incurred more debt. It's better to invest than gamble on the lottery. Saving even a little consistently for years will create wealth.

INSTANT SAVINGS USING STORE CREDIT CARDS

At least a couple of times a year, department stores push their credit cards with a teaser of 10% or more off on your store purchase if you sign up for their card. This sounds enticing, but could lead to a financial downfall. Here's why. The instant savings is a one-time good deal. A $100 purchase would result in an instant $10 savings, but, future purchases using the card would wipe out the instant savings because store cards usually have a higher interest rate than a bank charge card. An audit conducted by the U.S. House of Representatives in 2008 showed that the average store credit card rate was 22% to 28% while the bank card rate averaged 14%; that's an 8% to 14% difference. This rate difference can be costly if the balance is not paid in full each month. Also, store cards had a shorter grace period, the time when no interest was accrued. According to a Bank of America study, the average individual has eight store credit cards with balances. Are you one of them? What is the total balance on your store credit card debt? $_____

You can see from these few examples that *every penny counts*. It's up to you whether you spend money to create financial prosperity for others or save to create prosperity for yourself. I've shared the pitfalls of subprime and debt consolidation loans, playing the lottery, and the consequences of falling for instant IRS rebates, store credit cards, instant savings offers, and payday loans. Knowing the tools stores and banks use will result in better financial decisions.

TIPS AND TECHNIQUES TO SAVE $$$

I've shared some of the marketing techniques that keep you poor. Now I'd like to share some that can make you rich without making major changes in your lifestyle. I'll cover some techniques that aren't often discussed like making extra mortgage payments and refinancing your home.

MORTGAGE PAYMENTS

Becoming a homeowner is one of the American dreams and one of the most expensive. But, contrary to what most people do, a 30-year mortgage does not have to take 30 years to be home free. How much does a 30-year mortgage cost, and how can you save money and time to become title free?

A 30-year, $150,000 mortgage taken in May 2009 at a 4.5% interest rate results in 360, (12 X 30 = 360), monthly mortgage payments of $760.03 in principal and interest and a pay-off date of May 2039. Paying the note over the 30 years results in $123,607.23 in interest and a total cost of $273,610.80 (360 X $760.03) for the home. However, if you add a little extra to the principal, see how much money and time you can save (*Table 8-1*).

ACCELERATE PAYING OFF YOUR MORTGAGE

These calculations were added one on top of the other, but I hope you

EXTRA PAYMENT	$ INTEREST PAID	PAY-OFF DATE	TOTAL PAID FOR HOME
$0	$123,607.23	May 2039	$273,610.80
$25	$114,403.68	June 2037	$264,403.68
1 extra payment/year	$95,866.21	June 2033	$245,866.21
1 extra life of loan	$760.03	May 2033	$244,571.25

Table 8-1

see how much money and how much time you can save by just adding a little more to each of your payments over the life of your loan.

Now go one step further and add up how much money you can save over the life of the loan. Using the $25 per month example, you save $9,207.12 ($273,610.80 - $264,403.68) in interest and an additional $17,480.69 ($760.03 X 23) in mortgage payments. That's a total of $26,687.81 ($9,207.12 + $17,480.69) in savings!!!

It's easy and simple to add $25 more to a monthly payment. Twenty-five dollars a month could be one less meal eaten out, two fewer DVDs or CDs, one less movie at the theater, five days a month with coffee from home instead of at the office cafe or your local chain. You get the picture?

But you might be saying, "I had to come up with the extra $25 a month so I really didn't save a total of $26,687.81." Technically you're right. Adding the $25 extra a month costs you a total of $8,400 ($760.03 X 337 months) over the life of the loan. So, if you want to be precise, you saved only $10,807.12 ($19,207.12 - $8,400) over the life of the loan and you became mortgage free only 23 months earlier. Well, if 1,080,712 pennies saved isn't a lot to you, I'll take it any day!!! Because every penny counts!

Another savings technique is to secure a 15-year loan instead of the more common 30-year note. The mortgage payment of a 15-year loan would result in a monthly payment of $1147.49 in principal and interest. The total cost of the home would be $206,548 and 56,548.19 in interest. That's a savings of $67,061.88 in interest over the 30-year loan.

If you can't afford to pay the increased mortgage payment on a 15-year note, then just adding $100 to each monthly payment on a 30-

year mortgage would result in the loan being paid off 4 years earlier; that's 26 years instead of 30 years and results in a total interest of $194,404.22 over the life of the loan. You can also save by making one additional payment a year and pay only $191,154.87 in interest. That's pretty much what making bi-weekly payments does. Bottom line, anytime you increase your principal payment on a loan you reduce interest payments and time.

What this example shows that is the power is in your hands to control your financial destiny. Once you have the knowledge, you can decide how soon you want to be mortgage free and how much you need to add to your mortgage payment.

Remember our lesson on developing your spend plan? As you free up money by paying off debts, or rearrange your variable expenses, you can free up as much money as you need to pay your home off early.

REFINANCING YOUR HOME

When the budget is tight and interest rates are lower, it's not uncommon for mortgage lenders to encourage refinancing your home. There are many pros and cons that should be considered when you refinance. For example: many people look at the plus side of refinancing...the lower mortgage payment. However, many don't consider the one important negative side, and that is that they restart the clock by taking out another 30-year mortgage. I can't stress it enough, the shorter the payback period, the more you save. Since the borrower is slave to the lender…in this case you enter into 30 more years of slavery. When the additional 30-year refinance is added to the original loan period, the total cost of your home could be astronomical. Before refinancing your home, look at the total cost. That includes the total payment over the life of the loan; the principal, interest, all points and closing costs. Refinancing may free up money, but it may not be the best option available when the total cost of the new loan is considered. To maximize a home refinance, consider a loan of 15 years or the balance of your existing loan, i.e. 20 or 25 years. Many don't ask their lender for periods of less than 30 years but it is an option; just ask; you'll save time and money.

MORTGAGE/REFINANCE COMPARISON WORKSHEET

Company	Type	Loan Amount	Interest	Principal & Interest	Points	Origination	Total Closing	Total Loan Cost
ABC	15yr Con	$150,000	4.25	$1,128.42	2.5	1		$203,115
					$3,750	$1,500	$5,250	$208,365
ABC	15yr Con	$150,000	4.5	$1,147.49	1.25	1		$206,548
					$1,875	$1,500	$3,375	$209,923
ABC	15yr VA	$150,000	4.25	$1,128.42	1	1		$203,115
					$1,500	$1,500	$3,000	$206,115
ABC	30yr Con	$150,000	4.5	$760.03	1	0		$273,610
					$1,500	0	$1,500	$275,110
ABC	30yr VA	$150,000	4.75	$782.47	0.75	1		$281,689
					$1,125	$1,500	$2,625	$284,314

Table 8-2

Another key point in refinancing your home is to research for the best interest rate; however, once again consider the total cost of the loan. Ask each lender for various options; VA, FHA, Conventional, 15 years, 20 years, 25 years, etc. Create a comparison matrix so that you base your refinancing decision on the numbers. I've included a sample on the previous page (see *Table 8-2)*.

Finally, don't go with just one quote from the lender. By this I mean call back and talk with several representatives from the lender to compare rates. When I was refinancing our home to get a reduced rate, I worked with our broker who only dealt with "exclusive candidates" because we were supposed to receive the "best rate". To ensure her rate was the best, after we received her rate, I called the company's Customer Service Representative in the Mortgage Department. What I learned from my research was our broker quoted us a rate that was 1.5% lower than the Service Representative quoted. The difference in the rates quoted to me was a difference of $21,095.55 in interest over the life of the loan! Lenders have a "spread" that they allow various representatives to use. Work to get the best rate, because once you sign the loan papers, you're committed. We didn't refinance with our existing lender because we received a better rate from one of their competitors. **Always, always do your homework before you sign the papers.**

INVEST TO BUILD WEALTH

The wise man plans now and saves for the future,
but the foolish person squanders what he has.
- Proverbs 21:20 (NIV, Message, Amplified)

I've talked about where you're spending your money, how to budget and become debt free, and some of the tricks, traps, and techniques companies use to get your money. Now let's focus on how to build wealth from the hundreds and thousands of pennies you've saved by applying what you've learned.

My goal is not to make you an investment pro, but to educate you on the investment options available to you. Once you've determined your one, three, and five year financial goals, it's easy to reduce the goal to a dollar figure using the numerous financial calculators at the various web sites. The challenge will be to invest consistently to reach your objective.

I tried for years to get my daughter to invest but she always felt overwhelmed by the complexity of the investment industry. It was difficult for me to understand her reluctance since she's smart and disciplined in every other area of her life. After listening to her complaints and those of my students, I began to understand why people are sometimes scared to invest. People in the investment business have a language of their own and they can make investing seem complicated; but it's not. I hope to demystify it for you.

I am not an investment professional. Therefore, I will not give you advice on where to invest. What I will provide to you is some investing guidelines, terminology, and options. Let's begin with some investing guidelines.

Guideline 1: You have to invest to create wealth. You can't create wealth over a lifetime if you put your savings in a bank savings account or a bank certificate of deposit. These are good for short term financial goals but don't produce enough interest to create the growth we've been talking about throughout this book. You must earn enough interest to beat inflation and maintain buying power. Savings accounts and bank certificates of deposit usually pay less than 3% which doesn't generate enough interest to create wealth.

Guideline 2: If you don't understand the investment, don't invest. Don't be afraid to say "I don't understand, please explain it to me." You've worked too hard for your money to let a broker or banker convince you to put your money into a product you don't fully understand…even if the investment has a potential to generate great returns. Notice I said "could" and not "will". There are no guarantees in the investment arena.

Over the course of our investing lifetime we've been involved in instruments we didn't understand because of the promise of high profits and tax benefits, only to find out the returns didn't materialize. Go slowly and invest wisely, read, read, read, and ask lots of questions along the way. If your agent can't fully explain the numbers, then wait and don't invest until he/she can and you feel comfortable the investment meets your financial objectives.

Here are some questions you should ask:

1. If I invest in this product, how much of my money will be invested? This is not a trick question. Here's why. There are fees attached to most, if not all, investment products. Some fees are up front, some are tacked on the back, and some are charged throughout the year. If, for example, you invest $1000, ask how much of that will be applied to the investment and when?

2. Will there be other fees if you withdraw during a certain time?

3.   How are you, as my agent, paid? Do you get a commission every time I invest or are you salaried?

4.   Why did you recommend this investment? This question is important because some agents get paid commissions based on the investment instruments. Some recommendations are made because of the total amount you have invested not because it's the best investment for you. By this I mean if your total portfolio in worth $10,000 most companies will place you in a class or group of investments that would be different from a person that has a $100,000 or $1,000,000 portfolio. In addition, although there are thousands of investment options available on the open market to select from, most brokerage firms represent and sell a small portfolio of those investments. It's too difficult for them to pick and choose what's best for you individually, so they lump investors by portfolios.

Guideline 3: Diversify: Invest in several products and among several companies. Don't risk loosing all of your investment dollars by putting all of your money in one basket. This also includes your company's stock or stock fund. I especially want to caution you about putting too much of your retirement funds in your company. Remember Enron? Diversifying also means don't spread your investments among too many products because it will be difficult for you to manage. There are products like mutual funds that allow you to diversify without spreading yourself thin.

Guideline 4: Don't follow the crowd. Check your sources/seek wise counsel. It's easy to want to follow celebrity, investment gurus, and financial magazines investment advice, but be careful! I've seen celebrities endorse investments that are near their profit peak or the company has falsified their assets. This caused a financial disaster. Just like you would ask your financial advisor how she/he is paid and her/his track record, apply the same questions to endorsements. I've followed articles in magazines that advise to invest in a product that has consistently lost money or produced less than stellar returns. Why did they do that; because the investment company was an advertiser, thus an investor, with the magazine. The same applies to television investment programs. The investment companies pay some of the personalities; they get commissions or investment products at a reduced cost because of their recommendations. I cannot stress enough the importance of researching each product to ensure **it fits your investment objectives** before you invest.

I've given you some investment guidelines, now let's cover a few investment terms. There are many internet resources available to you to help you understand investing. Do not be intimidated. Use internet search engines to your advantage to understand investing and the investment world. I found these investment definitions on the internet at Wikipedia and Investor Words. If I have not covered a term you're interested in, the internet is a great resource to use at your leisure.

Annual percentage of rate (APR), nominal APR, and **effective APR (EAR)** describe the interest rate for a whole year (annualized), rather than just a monthly fee/rate, as applied on a loan, mortgage, credit card, etc. It is a finance charge expressed as an annual rate.

Broker: A fee charged by a broker or agent for his/her service in facilitating a transaction, such as the buying or selling of securities or real estate. In the case of securities trading, brokers can be split into two broad categories depending on the commissions they charge. Discount brokers charge relatively low commissions, but provide no services beyond executing trades. Full service brokers charge higher commissions, but provide research and investment advisory services.

Commission: a fee charged by a broker for the services performed, usually buying or selling stocks, bonds, mutual funds, etc. A percentage of the money invested will be taken off the top to pay commissions.

Compound interest: the concept of adding accumulated interest back to the principal, so that interest is earned on interest from that moment on.

Credit score: a numerical expression based on a statistical analysis of a person's credit files, to represent the creditworthiness of that person. A credit score is primarily based on credit report information, typically sourced from credit bureaus.

FDIC: Federal Deposit Insurance Corporation. A federal agency that insures deposits in member banks and thrifts up to $200,000.

Fund: An investment company or mutual fund.

Fund family: A mutual fund company offering many mutual funds, for various objectives. Usually, investors can move assets between different funds of a family of funds at little or no cost, and can receive a single statement describing their holdings in all the funds in the family of funds; **also called** mutual fund family or fund family.

Interest: The interest rate is the yearly price charged by a lender to a borrower in order for the borrower to obtain a loan. This is usually expressed as a percentage of the total amount loaned.

Load: A sales charge added to the purchase and/or sale price of some mutual funds and annuities; the opposite of no-load.

Money Market Fund: a deposit account with a relatively high rate of interest and short notice (or no notice) required for withdrawals.

Portfolio: A collection of investments all owned by the same individual or organization. These investments often include stocks, which are investments in individual businesses; bonds, which are investments in debt that are designed to earn interest; and mutual funds, which are essentially pools of money from many investors that are invested by professionals or according to indices.

Prime Rate: The prime rate of interest is a rate of interest that serves as a benchmark for most other loans in a country. The precise definition of prime rate differs from country to country. In the United States, the prime rate is the interest rate banks charge to large corporations for short-term loans.

Prospectus: A legal document offering securities or mutual fund shares for sale, required by the Securities Act of 1933. It must explain the offer, including the terms, issuer, objectives (if mutual fund) or planned use of the money (if securities), historical financial statements, and other information that could help an individual decide whether the investment is appropriate for him/her.

Sales charge: A fee charged by a broker or agent for his/her service in facilitating a transaction.

SEC: Securities and Exchange Commission. The primary federal regulatory agency for the securities industry, whose responsibility is to promote full disclosure and to protect investors against fraudulent and manipulative practices in the securities markets.

Security: An investment instrument, other than an insurance policy or fixed annuity, issued by a corporation, government, or other organization which offers evidence of debt or equity.

Subprime rate: A financial term that was popularized by the media during the credit crunch of 2008 and involves financial institutions lending in ways which do not meet "prime" standards to an extent which puts the loans into the riskiest category of consumer loans typically sold in the secondary market. Although there is no single, standard definition, in the US subprime loans are usually classified as those where the borrower has a FICO score below 640.

12(b-1) fees: An extra fee charged by some mutual funds to cover promotion, distributions, marketing expenses, and sometimes commissions to brokers. A genuine no-load fund does not have Rule 12b-1 fees, although some funds calling themselves "no-load" do have Rule 12b-1 fees (as do some load funds). Rule 12b-1 fee information is disclosed in a fund's prospectus, is included in the stated expense ratio, and is usually less than 1%.

Trade/transaction: An agreement between a buyer and a seller to exchange an asset for payment.

Let's switch gears and cover investment options. As I said earlier, there are thousands of investment options available to you. One of the guiding principle of investing is to remember, the greater the potential for earnings the greater the risk of losing your initial investment. Also, with each investment, always factor in how additional costs and fees affect your return. It's material if an investment produces 8% returns when you have to pay 2-3% in costs and fees. I'll cover investment options starting with the least risky. I'll limit my discussion to the most common investments such as savings accounts, money market deposit accounts, mutual funds, stocks, and bonds.

Savings accounts are offered by banks and credit unions and usually offer low interest rates for two reasons. First, the rate is lower because you can withdraw your funds at any time, and secondly, the rate is low because there is little risk of losing your money. Savings accounts can be used to introduce your children to the concept of savings and for short-term savings. Always ensure your savings account is in a Federal Deposit Insurance Corporation (FDIC) institution. FDIC insures the safety of your funds up to $250,000 if there is mismanagement in the institution.

Money market deposit accounts (MMDA) are offered by banks, credit unions, and investment brokers. The best way to explain the difference between a money market deposit account and a savings account is that the MMDA is like a savings account on steroids. The interest rate is usually 1 to 2 percentage points higher. The minimum amount that has to be maintained in the account is higher, and although there may be check-writing privileges, there is a limited number of checks that can be written during a specified period of time. I recommend MMDAs as a place to keep emergency funds if you are able to meet the minimum balance required. Like the savings account, the MMDA is FDIC-insured.

Bonds are a loan to the institution/company issuing the bond. Bonds may be issued by banks, corporations, municipalities, the federal government, and investment brokers. The company agrees to pay you back the amount you loaned them plus an agreed interest rate. However, since bonds guarantee no loss of the initial investment, don't assume investing in bonds is risk free. With "callable" bonds there is the risk of loss of interest. If interest rates go down, the

112

institution may have the right to "call" or redeem your bond to save themselves money. On the opposite side, if rates go up, you may not have the right to cash in your bond to invest in a product that offers a higher return.

Mutual funds pool money from many investors to invest in stocks, bonds, and other securities. Mutual funds provide instant diversification, affordability, and professional management, however, these advantages come at a cost; e.g. management fees, sales charges, purchase fees, operating expenses, and many more. These fees, expenses, and charges must be factored when historical and projected returns are evaluated. Most mutual funds fall into one of three categories: 1) **money market funds**, 2) **bonds funds** and 3) **stock funds** which provide many investment options, I'll address them next.

Money market funds are different from money market deposit accounts because it is a type of mutual fund that is required by the Securities and Exchange Commission to invest in high quality short-term securities and pay dividends.

Bond funds are a higher risk than money market funds because their investment strategy is to produce high yields. Since the SEC does not restrict investment products for bond funds, it's important to research the company and the company's credit rating before investing. Bonds that promise a high rate of return, like junk bonds, should be a rarity in your investment portfolio.

Stock funds have historically produced the greatest investment rewards. However, just as stocks can fluctuate in price, a portfolio of stocks will fluctuate also. There are many types of stock funds to choose from: 1) **growth funds** invest in stocks that have the potential for large capital gains, 2) **income funds** invest in stocks that pay dividends, 3) **index funds** focus on a specific market or industry such as the Dow Jones, S&P 500, Wilshire 5000 Index, etc. and 4) **sector funds** which invest in specific industries like technology, medical, etc.

Stocks represent a share of ownership in a company. Most people don't realize that when they purchase stocks, they purchase them from the secondary market, which means the stocks are being purchased from someone other than the company. This is important because stocks gain some of their value from investor perception or expectation of the companies' future growth. The value of a stock can skyrocket from the announcement of a new product or plummet from the news of corrupt management.

Market analysts and investment professionals continually state "the stock market as a whole has produced returns of 10% or greater and therefore is a wise and safe investment." Likewise, they caution, "you can not time the market". My advice when buying stocks is: 1) research the company's financial statements to determine how they are managing debt and company growth, 2) study the company's historical performance and compare it against the performance of other companies in the same industry. Determine whether the company is leading the pack, in the middle, or at the bottom, 3) determine the stock price relative to its historical highs and lows. If the stock price is close to the high, determine if it will go higher or lower. In most instances, don't buy stocks at the high.

Before closing this chapter, there are a few words of caution I'd like to leave with you. No investment is risk-free and historical returns are not a guarantee for future gains. Fully understand the investment, the risks, and the costs before investing. Although you must invest to create and maintain wealth, taking short cuts through unscrupulous investing usually results in financial disaster. If a proposal seems too good to be true, it usually is. Do your homework and don't trust "just anyone" with your hard-earned money. Finally, once you invest you can't forget about your investments. The market changes constantly and changes in your lifestyle may dictate changes in your investment goals, horizons, and choices.

NO MORE EXCUSES

I hope this book has been helpful. My intent was not to make you feel victimized, or foolish, or angry. It was to educate; because once you know better, you do better. Now that you have knowledge, stop making excuses and make changes to achieve financial success. I'd like to summarize the key points of this book before we close.

❖ **Plan and then spend.** Don't rush to spend; plan and make your money work as hard for you as you worked for it.

❖ **The power of compounding.** Interest rates are important, regardless of whether you earn it on your investment or pay it on a loan. Compounding is a mathematical explosion. Money grows faster the more it's compounded and the longer it's invested.

❖ **Count the cost.** Don't ask about payments, ask how much. Know the total cost to you in dollars, time, and annual interest rates. Budget for your purchases and pay cash as often as possible. Pay credit card balances in full and on time.

❖ **Budget is not a bad word.** Having a budget ensures you reach your financial goals. Know how you will spend your paycheck before you receive it and balance to zero, on paper, each month. Track you expenses on the Spending Tracker and you'll see yourself making progress to becoming a middle-income millionaire.

❖ **Don't get ripped off.** Know the terms of a contract before you sign. Once you sign, you've lost your leverage to negotiate. There are many scams, frauds, swindles, shams, and outright criminal tactics being used to get your money. Some of them include payday loans, rent-to-own, same as cash, instant tax rebates, etc. Be patient and disciplined. It will save you money.

❖ **Apply the Tips and Techniques to save $$$.** There are many tactics available to continue your lifestyle and save money. Some include paying your mortgage, credit cards and loans off early. Be aware of the pitfalls of debt consolidation and sub-prime loans. Know the total price before entering into a contractual agreement.

❖ **Little by little, make it grow.** You must invest to achieve financial wealth. Invest consistently and automatically. Fancy investments do not guarantee financial rewards. Before you invest, know how the investment fits into your financial objectives; know the total cost in fees and penalties. Know how the brokerage or banking firm compensates the investment agent. Reduce your risk by diversifying your investments to several types and several companies. Monitor your investments to achieve your financial objectives. Don't fall for the get rich quick schemes. They don't work.

❖ **Seek wise counsel and ask many questions.** If it sounds too good to be true, usually it is.

❖ **Focus on the finish line.** You may have setbacks along your journey to financial wealth, but stay in the race and focus on your finish line. You don't have to be a financial genius to make and save money. You don't have to be rich to become rich, and you don't have to have a lot of money to make money. These are myths that have kept most of us poor. Change your habits and have a financially prosperous life.

❖ **Every Penny Count$.** Remember, the borrower is slave to the lender. The more you borrow, the poorer you become and the longer you live in financial bondage. Bondage disrupts and destroys your family, your future, your health and peace of mind. Most purchases are consumable items, which will be replaced in five years or less. This includes cars, electronics, clothes, vacations, etc. There's always an "it" item that's newer, better, bigger, or greater. Is getting "it" costing you your financial wealth?

Managing money reminds me of the biblical principal of the law of the harvest from Galatians, chapter six, verse seven (b): *for whatever a man sows, this he will also reap (New American Standard Bible)*. I learned four lessons from this scripture that I want to share with you.

Lesson 1: You reap if you sow: you have to delay spending now to reap/achieve wealth later.

Lesson 2: You reap what you sow: if you chose wise investments you will reap solid financial returns; there is no shortcut to long-term wealth.

Lesson 3: You reap after you sow: the sooner you invest and the longer you invest, the greater amount you will reap.

Lesson 4: You reap more than you sow: the power of time, interest, and compounding will help you reap more than you invested; even a little invested consistently can become a lot over time.

I have given you the facts, statistics, and principles of achieving financial wealth. Now it's up to you to apply them. You have no more excuses.

SAVINGS AND INVESTMENT WEBSITES

www.bankrate.com: Contains excellent budget and calculator tools that allow you to plan for retirement, education funding, mortgage, and loan repayments.

www.myfico.com: Provides free calculator to estimate your FICO score. Payment is required to get your official FICO score.

www.cnnmoney.com: Contains calculators, financial updates, investment tracker, up-to-date information on market trends, and financial education tools.

www.kiplinger.com: On-line personal finance and business site which includes articles, market trends and recommendations, and financial calculators.

www.annualcreditreport.com: Government sponsored program that allows three free credit reports annually. A report can be obtained from each of the credit reporting agencies; Experian, Transunion and Equifax annually.

121

MARY AND JOHN ROBINSON'S BUDGET
As of 1 Jan 2009

CATEGORIES	TOTAL	1ST	2ND	CATEGORY TOTAL
1. GIVING				
TITHE/OFFERING	330	165	165	
GIVING				330
2. HOUSING				
MORTGAGE	2000	1000	1000	
ELECTRIC	200	200	0	
CELL PHONES	160	0	160	
CABLE	100	100	0	
WATER*	32	0	32	
HOA	41	41	0	
SECURITY	41	0	41	
MAINTENANCE*	200	100	100	
				2774
3. FOOD	250	125	125	
				250
4. TRANSPORTATION				
PAYMENT	430	0	430	
GAS	160	80	80	
TAGS/INSPTS*	15	0	15	
INSURANCE*	30	0	30	
MAINTENANCE*	50	0	50	
				685
5. HEALTH				
MEDICAL CO-PAY	30	30	0	
DENTAL CO-PAY*	15	0	15	
DISABILITY	39	0	39	
LIFE INSURANCE	39	0	39	
				123
TOTAL				4162

Variable expenses * $612

SALARY $70,816   TAKE HOME PAY $4,818

CATEGORIES	TOTAL	1ST	2ND	CATEGORY TOTAL
6. CLOTHING				
PURCHASES*	20	10	10	
DRY CLEANING	6	0	6	
				26
7. ENTERTAINMENT				
MOVIES	10	5	5	
EATING AT WORK	50	25	25	
				60
8. RECREATION				
VACATIONS*	200	100	100	
JUDO LESSONS	60	30	30	
				260
9. MISCELLANEOUS				
SALON/HAIR CUTS	80	40	40	
				80
10. ALLOWANCE				
ADULTS	50	25	25	
				50
11. SUBSCRIPTION				
NEWSPAPER	15	15	0	
				15
12. GIFTS*	50	25	25	
				50
13. INVESTMENTS				
SAVINGS	50	25	25	
401(k)	0	0	0	
RETIREMENT	0	0	0	
				50
14. DEBTS	BALANCE	MINIMUM PAY		
MACY'S	200	15	0	
CAPITAL ONE	1000	50	0	
				65
TOTAL				656	4818

FirstFruits Ministry © 1982

FINANCIAL PLAN FOR

CATEGORIES	TOTAL	1ST	2ND	CATEGORY TOTAL
1. GIVING				
TITHE/OFFERING				
GIVING				
2. HOUSING				
MORTGAGE				
ELECTRIC				
WATER				
TELEPHONE				
CELL PHONE				
INSURANCE				
CABLE				
REPAIRS*				
HOA				
OTHER				
OTHER				
3. FOOD				
GROCERY				
4. AUTOMOBILE				
PAYMENT				
GAS				
TAGS/INSPTS*				
INSURANCE				
REPAIRS &				
TIRES*				
5. HEALTH				
DISABILITY				
MEDICAL				
DR VISITS				
TOTAL				

Variable expenses *

SALARY _____   TAKE HOME PAY _____

CATEGORIES	TOTAL	1ST	2ND	CATEGORY TOTAL	
6. CLOTHING					
PURCHASES*					
DRY CLEANING					
7. ENTERTAINMENT					
RESTAURANT					
MISCELLANEOUS					
OTHER					
8. RECREATION					
VACATION					
OTHER					
9. MISCELLANEOUS					
SALON/HAIR					
MISCELLANEOUS					
MISCELLANEOUS					
10. ALLOWANCE					
ADULTS					
11. SUBSCRIPTION					
NEWSPAPER					
12. GIFTS/CHRISTMAS*					
13. INVESTMENTS					
SAVINGS					
14. DEBT					
CREDIT CARD					
CREDIT CARD					
CREDIT CARD					
CREDIT CARD					
TOTAL					

FirstFruits Ministry © 1982

SPENDING TRACKER

CATEGORIES	TOTAL	JAN	FEB	MAR	APR	MAY	JUN
1. GIVING							
TITHE/OFFERING							
GIVING							
2. HOUSING							
MORTGAGE							
ELECTRIC							
CELL PHONES							
CABLE							
WATER*							
HOA							
SECURITY							
MISCELLANEOUS*							
3. FOOD							
4. AUTOMOBILE							
PAYMENT							
GAS							
TAGS/INSPTS*							
INSURANCE*							
MAINTENANCE*							
5. HEALTH							
MEDICAL CO-PAY							
DENTAL CO-PAY*							
DISABILITY							
LIFE INSURANCE							
6. CLOTHING							
PURCHASES*							
DRY CLEANING							
7. ENTERTAINMENT							
DINING OUT							
OTHER							
8. RECREATION							
VACATIONS*							
OTHER							
9. MISCELLANEOUS							
SALON/HAIR CUTS							
10. ALLOWANCE							
ADULTS							
11. SUBSCRIPTION							
NEWSPAPER							
12. GIFTS*							
13. INVESTMENTS							
SAVINGS							
401(k)							
RETIREMENT							
14. DEBTS							
MISCELLANEOUS							
MISCELLANEOUS							
TOTAL							

AS OF _____

CATEGORIES	TOTAL	JUL	AUG	SEP	OCT	NOV	DEC
1. GIVING							
TITHE/OFFERING							
GIVING							
2. HOUSING							
MORTGAGE							
ELECTRIC							
CELL PHONES							
CABLE							
WATER*							
HOA							
SECRUITY							
MISCELLANEOUS*							
3. FOOD							
4. AUTOMOBILE							
PAYMENT							
GAS							
TAGS/INSPTS*							
INSURANCE*							
MAINTENANCE*							
5. HEALTH							
MEDICAL CO-PAY							
DENTAL CO-PAY*							
DISABILITY							
LIFE INSURANCE							
6. CLOTHING							
PURCHASES*							
DRY CLEANING							
7. ENTERTAINMENT							
DINING OUT							
OTHER							
8. RECREATION							
VACATIONS*							
OTHER							
9. MISCELLANEOUS							
SALON/HAIR CUTS							
10. ALLOWANCE							
ADULTS							
11. SUBSCRIPTION							
NEWSPAPER							
12. GIFTS*							
13. INVESTMENTS							
SAVINGS							
401(k)							
RETIREMENT							
14. DEBTS							
MISCELLANEOUS							
MISCELLANEOUS							
TOTAL							

SAMPLE DEBT REDUCTION PLAN

#1 #3

DEBTS	BAL	MIN	JAN	FEB	MAR	APR	MAY	JUN
JO'S BOUTIQUE	$250	$20	$250	$0	$0	$0	$0	$0
MONEY STORE	$400	$20	$400	$0	$0	$0	$0	$0
QUICK CASH	$1,479	$100	$102	$752	$625	$0	$0	$0
CREDIT CARD #1 HIS	$3,700	$0	$0	$0	$127	$752	$2,821	$0
READY MONEY	$4,000	$50	$50	$50	$50	$50	$ 4,000	$0
CREDIT CARD #2 HERS	$4,562	$0	$0	$0	$0	$0	$4,562	$0
STUDENT LOAN	$5,000	$60	$60	$60	$60	$60	$1,169	$862
GOOD NEIGHBORS BANK	$9,925	$0	$0	$0	$0	$0	$0	$0
CREDIT UNION	$10,596	$300	$300	$300	$300	$300	$300	$300
BANK LINE OF CREDIT	$22,840	$78	$78	$78	$78	$78	$78	$78
HOSPITAL	$27,533	$620	$620	$620	$620	$620	$620	$620
TOTAL DEBT	$90,285	$1,248	$1,860	$1,860	$1,860	$1,860	$13,550	$1,860

#2 #4

Freed up $1,860 for debt reduction
* May will receive 3 paychecks and tax refund = $11,690
** Oct will receive 3 paychecks = $5,040

DEBTS	BAL	MIN	JUL	AUG	SEP	OCT	NOV	DEC
JO'S BOUTIQUE	$0	$0	$0	$0	$0	$0	$0	$0
MONEY STORE	$0	$0	$0	$0	$0	$0	$0	$0
QUICK CASH	$0	$0	$0	$0	$0	$0	$0	$0
CREDIT CARD #1 HIS	$0	$0	$0	$0	$0	$0	$0	$0
READY MONEY	$0	$0	$0	$0	$0	$0	$0	$0
CREDIT CARD #2 HERS	$0	$0	$0	$0	$0	$0	$0	$0
STUDENT LOAN	$2,669	$60	$862	$862	$862	$83	$0	$0
GOOD NEIGHBORS BANK	$9,925	$0	$0	$0	$0	$5,819	$862	$862
CREDIT UNION	$8,800	$300	$300	$300	$300	$300	$300	$300
BANK LINE OF CREDIT	$22,372	$78	$78	$78	$78	$78	$78	$78
HOSPITAL	$23,813	$620	$620	$620	$620	$620	$620	$620
TOTAL DEBT	$67,579	$1,058	$1,860	$1,860	$1,860	$6,900	$1,860	$1,860

FirstFruits Ministry © 2009

HOW TO CONSTRUCT A DEBT REDUCTION PLAN

1. List debts from the smallest to the largest balance; don't focus on minimum payments.

2. Determine the amount that will be freed up to pay down debt; in this case $1,860 per month.

3. Allocate dollars against the minimum balances first, then the remaining excess dollars to the smallest debt. In our example, the minimum balances total $1,248; the remaining $652 was allocated to the first three smallest debts.

4. Additional income streams, bonuses, refunds, additional paychecks, should be allocated to pay down debt. In May and Oct an additional $11,690 and $5,040 was received and used to pay debts.

5. Continue this process until all debts are paid. After becoming debt free, use freed up dollars to accomplish other financial goals, e.g. invest to build wealth, pay off home, fund college and/or retirement plans.

DEBT REDUCTION PLAN FOR

DEBTS	BAL	MIN	JAN	FEB	MAR	APR	MAY	JUN
1								
2								
3								
4								
5								
6								
7								
8								
9								
10								
TOTAL DEBT								

DEBTS	BAL	MIN	JUL	AUG	SEP	OCT	NOV	DEC
1								
2								
3								
4								
5								
6								
7								
8								
9								
10								
TOTAL DEBT